DASH COOKBOOK 2022

EFFORTLESS RECIPES TO LOWER BLOOD PRESSURE

MICHAEL THOMPSON

Table of Contents

Trout and Carrots Soup 12

Turkey and Fennel Stew 13

Eggplant Soup 14

Sweet Potatoes Cream 15

Chicken and Mushrooms Soup 16

Lime Salmon Pan 17

Potato Salad 18

Ground Beef and Tomato Pan 20

Shrimp and Avocado Salad 21

Broccoli Cream 22

Cabbage Soup 23

Celery and Cauliflower Soup 24

Pork and Leeks Soup 25

Minty Shrimp and Broccoli Salad 26

Shrimp and Cod Soup 27

Shrimp and Green Onions Mix 28

Spinach Stew 29

Curry Cauliflower Mix 30

Carrots and Zucchini Stew 31

Cabbage and Green Beans Stew 32

Chili Mushroom Soup 33

Chili Pork 34

Paprika Mushroom and Salmon Salad 35

Chickpeas and Potatoes Medley 36

Cardamom Chicken Mix	37
Lentils Chili	38
Rosemary Endives	39
Lemony Endives	40
Pesto Asparagus	41
Paprika Carrots	42
Creamy Potato Pan	43
Sesame Cabbage	44
Cilantro Broccoli	45
Chili Brussels Sprouts	46
Brussels Sprouts and Green Onions Mix	47
Mashed Cauliflower	48
Avocado Salad	49
Radish Salad	50
Lemony Endives Salad	51
Olives and Corn Mix	52
Arugula and Pine Nuts Salad	53
Almonds and Spinach	54
Green Beans and Corn Salad	55
Endives and Kale Salad	56
Edamame Salad	57
Grapes and Avocados Salad	58
Oregano Eggplant Mix	59
Baked Tomatoes Mix	60
Thyme Mushrooms	61
Spinach and Corn Sauté	62
Corn and Scallions Sauté	63

Spinach and Mango Salad	64
Mustard Potatoes	65
Coconut Brussels Sprouts	66
Sage Carrots	67
Garlic Mushrooms and Corn	68
Pesto Green Beans	69
Tarragon Tomatoes	70
Almond Beets	71
Minty Tomatoes and Corn	72
Zucchini and Avocado Salsa	73
Apples and Cabbage Mix	74
Roasted Beets	75
Dill Cabbage	76
Cabbage and Carrot Salad	77
Tomato and Olives Salsa	78
Zucchini Salad	79
Curry Carrots Slaw	80
Lettuce and Beet Salad	81
Herbed Radishes	82
Baked Fennel Mix	83
Roasted Peppers	84
Dates and Cabbage Sauté	85
Black Beans Mix	86
Olives and Endives Mix	87
Tomatoes and Cucumber Salad	88
Peppers and Carrot Salad	89
Black Beans and Rice Mix	90

Rice and Cauliflower Mix	91
Balsamic Beans Mix	92
Creamy Beets	93
Avocado and Bell Peppers Mix	94
Roasted Sweet Potato and Beets	95
Kale Sauté	96
Spiced Carrots	97
Lemony Artichokes	98
Broccoli, Beans and Rice	99
Baked Squash Mix	100
Creamy Asparagus	101
Basil Turnips Mix	102
Rice and Capers Mix	103
Spinach and Kale Mix	104
Shrimp and Pineapple mix	105
Salmon and Green Olives	106
Salmon and Fennel	107
Cod and Asparagus	108
Spiced Shrimp	109
Sea Bass and Tomatoes	110
Shrimp and Beans	111
Shrimp and Horseradish Mix	112
Shrimp and Tarragon Salad	113
Parmesan Cod Mix	114
Tilapia and Red Onion Mix	115
Trout Salad	116
Balsamic Trout	117

Parsley Salmon	118
Trout and Veggie Salad	119
Saffron Salmon	120
Shrimp and Watermelon Salad	121
Oregano Shrimp and Quinoa Salad	122
Crab Salad	123
Balsamic Scallops	124
Creamy Flounder Mix	125
Spicy Salmon and Mango Mix	126
Dill Shrimp Mix	127
Salmon Pate	128
Shrimp with Artichokes	129
Shrimp with Lemon Sauce	130
Tuna and Orange Mix	131
Salmon Curry	132
Salmon and Carrots Mix	133
Shrimp and Pine Nuts Mix	134
Chili Cod and Green Beans	135
Garlic Scallops	136
Creamy Sea Bass Mix	137
Sea Bass and Mushrooms Mix	138
Salmon Chowder	139
Nutmeg Shrimp	140
Shrimp and Berries Mix	141
Baked Lemony Trout	142
Chives Scallops	143
Tuna Meatballs	144

Salmon Pan ... 145

Mustard Cod Mix ... 146

Shrimp and Asparagus Mix ... 147

Cod and Peas ... 148

Shrimp and Mussels Bowls ... 149

Dash Diet Dessert Recipes ... 150

Mint Cream ... 151

Raspberries Pudding ... 152

Almond Bars ... 153

Baked Peaches Mix ... 154

Walnuts Cake ... 155

Apple Cake ... 156

Cinnamon Cream ... 157

Creamy Strawberries Mix ... 158

Vanilla Pecan Brownies ... 159

Strawberries Cake ... 160

Cocoa Pudding ... 162

Nutmeg Vanilla Cream ... 163

Avocado Cream ... 164

Raspberries Cream ... 165

Watermelon Salad ... 166

Coconut Pears Mix ... 167

Apples Compote ... 168

Apricots Stew ... 169

Lemon Cantaloupe Mix ... 170

Creamy Rhubarb Cream ... 171

Pineapple Bowls ... 172

Blueberry Stew	173
Lime Pudding	174
Peach Cream	175
Cinnamon Plums Mix	176
Chia and Vanilla Apples	177
Rice and Pears Pudding	178
Rhubarb Stew	179
Rhubarb Cream	180
Blueberries Salad	181
Dates and Banana Cream	182
Plum Muffins	183
Plums and Raisins Bowls	184
Sunflower Seed Bars	185
Blackberries and Cashews Bowls	186
Orange and Mandarins Bowls	187
Pumpkin Cream	188
Figs and Rhubarb Mix	189
Spiced Banana	190
Cocoa Smoothie	191
Banana Bars	192
Green Tea and Dates Bars	193
Walnut Cream	194
Lemon Cake	195
Raisins Bars	196
Nectarines Squares	197
Grapes Stew	198
Mandarin and Plums Cream	199

Cherry and Strawberries Cream 200

Cardamom Walnuts and Rice Pudding 201

Pears Bread 202

Rice and Cherries Pudding 203

Watermelon Stew 204

Ginger Pudding 205

Cashew Cream 206

Hemp Cookies 207

Almonds and Pomegranate Bowls 208

Chicken Thighs and Rosemary Veggies 209

Chicken with Carrots and Cabbage 210

Eggplant and Turkey Sandwich 211

Simple Turkey and Zucchini Tortillas 213

Chicken with Peppers and Eggplant Pan 214

Balsamic Baked Turkey 215

Cheddar Turkey Mix 216

Parmesan Turkey 217

Creamy Chicken and Shrimp Mix 218

Basil Turkey and Hot Asparagus Mix 219

Trout and Carrots Soup

Preparation time: 10 minutes
Cooking time: 25 minutes
Servings: 4

Ingredients:
- 1 yellow onion, chopped
- 12 cups low-sodium fish stock
- 1 pound carrots, sliced
- 1 pound trout fillets, boneless, skinless and cubed
- 1 tablespoon sweet paprika
- 1 cup tomatoes, cubed
- 1 tablespoon olive oil
- Black pepper to the taste

Directions:
1. Heat up a pot with the oil over medium-high heat, add the onion, stir and sauté for 5 minutes.
2. Add the fish, carrots and the rest of the ingredients, bring to a simmer and cook over medium heat for 20 minutes.
3. Ladle the soup into bowls and serve.

Nutrition: calories 361, fat 13.4, fiber 4.6, carbs 164, protein 44.1

Turkey and Fennel Stew

Preparation time: 10 minutes
Cooking time: 45 minutes
Servings: 4

Ingredients:
- 1 turkey breast, skinless, boneless and cubed
- 2 fennel bulbs, sliced
- 1 tablespoon olive oil
- 2 bay leaves
- 1 yellow onion, chopped
- 1 cup canned tomatoes, no-salt-added
- 2 low-sodium beef stock
- 3 garlic cloves, chopped
- Black pepper to the taste

Directions:
1. Heat up a pan with the oil over medium heat, add the onion and the meat and brown for 5 minutes.
2. Add the fennel and the rest of the ingredients, bring to a simmer and cook over medium heat for 40 minutes, stirring from time to time.
3. Divide the stew into bowls and serve.

Nutrition: calories 371, fat 12.8, fiber 5.3, carbs 16.7, protein 11.9

Eggplant Soup

Preparation time: 10 minutes
Cooking time: 30 minutes
Servings: 4

Ingredients:
- 2 big eggplants, roughly cubed
- 1 quart low-sodium veggie stock
- 2 tablespoons no-salt-added tomato paste
- 1 red onion, chopped
- 1 tablespoon olive oil
- 1 tablespoon cilantro, chopped
- A pinch of black pepper

Directions:
1. Heat up a pot with the oil over medium heat, add the onion, stir and sauté for 5 minutes.
2. Add the eggplants and the other ingredients, bring to a simmer over medium heat, cook for 25 minutes, divide into bowls and serve.

Nutrition: calories 335, fat 14.4, fiber 5, carbs 16.1, protein 8.4

Sweet Potatoes Cream

Preparation time: 10 minutes
Cooking time: 25 minutes
Servings: 4

Ingredients:
- 4 cups veggie stock
- 2 tablespoons avocado oil
- 2 sweet potatoes, peeled and cubed
- 2 yellow onions, chopped
- 2 garlic cloves, minced
- 1 cup coconut milk
- A pinch of black pepper
- ½ teaspoon basil, chopped

Directions:
1. Heat up a pot with the oil over medium heat, add the onion and the garlic, stir and sauté for 5 minutes.
2. Add the sweet potatoes and the rest of the ingredients, bring to a simmer and cook over medium heat for 20 minutes.
3. Blend the soup using an immersion blender, ladle into bowls and serve for lunch.

Nutrition: calories 303, fat 14.4, fiber 4, carbs 9.8, protein 4.5

Chicken and Mushrooms Soup

Preparation time: 10 minutes
Cooking time: 30 minutes
Servings: 4

Ingredients:
- 1 quart veggie stock, low-sodium
- 1 tablespoon ginger, grated
- 1 yellow onion, chopped
- 1 tablespoon olive oil
- 1 pound chicken breast, skinless, boneless and cubed
- ½ pound white mushrooms, sliced
- 4 Thai chilies, chopped
- ¼ cup lime juice
- ¼ cup cilantro, chopped
- A pinch of black pepper

Directions:
1. Heat up a pot with the oil over medium heat, add the onion, ginger, chilies and the meat, stir and brown for 5 minutes.
2. Add the mushrooms, stir and cook for 5 minutes more.
3. Add the rest of the ingredients, bring to a simmer and cook over medium heat for 20 minutes more.
4. Ladle the soup into bowls and serve right away.

Nutrition: calories 226, fat 8.4, fiber 3.3, carbs 13.6, protein 28.2

Lime Salmon Pan

Preparation time: 10 minutes
Cooking time: 20 minutes
Servings: 4

Ingredients:
- 4 salmon fillet, boneless
- 3 garlic cloves, minced
- 1 yellow onion, chopped
- Black pepper to the taste
- 2 tablespoons olive oil
- Juice of 1 lime
- 1 tablespoon lime zest, grated
- 1 tablespoon thyme, chopped

Directions:
1. Heat up a pan with the oil over medium-high heat, add the onion and garlic, stir and sauté for 5 minutes.
2. Add the fish and cook it for 3 minutes on each side.
3. Add the rest of the ingredients, cook everything for 10 minutes more, divide between plates and serve for lunch.

Nutrition: calories 315, fat 18.1, fiber 1.1, carbs 4.9, protein 35.1

Potato Salad

Preparation time: 10 minutes
Cooking time: 20 minutes
Servings: 4

Ingredients:
- 2 tomatoes, chopped
- 2 avocados, pitted and chopped
- 2 cups baby spinach
- 2 scallions, chopped
- 1 pound gold potatoes, boiled, peeled and cut into wedges
- 1 tablespoon olive oil
- 1 tablespoon lemon juice
- 1 yellow onion, chopped
- 2 garlic cloves, minced
- Black pepper to the taste
- 1 bunch cilantro, chopped

Directions:
1. Heat up a pan with the oil over medium-high heat, add the onion, scallions and the garlic, stir and sauté for 5 minutes.
2. Add the potatoes, toss gently and cook for 5 minutes more.
3. Add the rest of the ingredients, toss, cook over medium heat for 10 minutes more, divide into bowls and serve for lunch.

Nutrition: calories 342, fat 23.4, fiber 11.7, carbs 33.5, protein 5

Ground Beef and Tomato Pan

Preparation time: 10 minutes
Cooking time: 20 minutes
Servings: 4

Ingredients:
- 1 pound beef, ground
- 1 red onion, chopped
- 1 tablespoon olive oil
- 1 cup cherry tomatoes, halved
- ½ red bell pepper, chopped
- Black pepper to the taste
- 1 tablespoon chives, chopped
- 1 tablespoon rosemary, chopped
- 3 tablespoons low-sodium beef stock

Directions:
1. Heat up a pan with the oil over medium heat, add the onion and the bell pepper, stir and sauté for 5 minutes.
2. Add the meat, stir and brown it for another 5 minutes.
3. Add the rest of the ingredients, toss, cook for 10 minutes, divide into bowls and serve for lunch.

Nutrition: calories 320, fat 11.3, fiber 4.4, carbs 18.4, protein 9

Shrimp and Avocado Salad

Preparation time: 5 minutes
Cooking time: 0 minutes
Servings: 4

Ingredients:
- 1 orange, peeled and cut into segments
- 1 pound shrimp, cooked, peeled and deveined
- 2 cups baby arugula
- 1 avocado, pitted, peeled and cubed
- 2 tablespoons olive oil
- 2 tablespoons balsamic vinegar
- Juice of ½ orange
- Salt and black pepper

Directions:
1. In a salad bowl, mix combine the shrimp with the oranges and the other ingredients, toss and serve for lunch.

Nutrition: calories 300, fat 5.2, fiber 2, carbs 11.4, protein 6.7

Broccoli Cream

Preparation time: 10 minutes
Cooking time: 40 minutes
Servings: 4

Ingredients:
- 2 pounds broccoli florets
- 1 yellow onion, chopped
- 1 tablespoon olive oil
- Black pepper to the taste
- 2 garlic cloves, minced
- 3 cups low-sodium beef stock
- 1 cup coconut milk
- 2 tablespoons cilantro, chopped

Directions:
1. Heat up a pot with the oil over medium heat, add the onion and the garlic, stir and sauté for 5 minutes.
2. Add the broccoli and the other ingredients except the coconut milk, bring to a simmer and cook over medium heat for 35 minutes more.
3. Blend the soup using an immersion blender, add the coconut milk, pulse again, divide into bowls and serve.

Nutrition: calories 330, fat 11.2, fiber 9.1, carbs 16.4, protein 9.7

Cabbage Soup

Preparation time: 10 minutes
Cooking time: 40 minutes
Servings: 4

Ingredients:
- 1 big green cabbage head, roughly shredded
- 1 yellow onion, chopped
- 1 tablespoon olive oil
- Black pepper to the taste
- 1 leek, chopped
- 2 cups canned tomatoes, low-sodium
- 4 cups chicken stock, low-sodium
- 1 tablespoon cilantro, chopped

Directions:
1. Heat up a pot with the oil over medium heat, add the onion and the leek, stir and cook for 5 minutes.
2. Add the cabbage and the rest of the ingredients except the cilantro, bring to a simmer and cook over medium heat for 35 minutes.
3. Ladle the soup into bowls, sprinkle the cilantro on top and serve.

Nutrition: calories 340, fat 11.7, fiber 6, carbs 25.8, protein 11.8

Celery and Cauliflower Soup

Preparation time: 10 minutes
Cooking time: 40 minutes
Servings: 4

Ingredients:
- 2 pounds cauliflower florets
- 1 red onion, chopped
- 1 tablespoon olive oil
- 1 cup tomato puree
- Black pepper to the taste
- 1 cup celery, chopped
- 6 cups low-sodium chicken stock
- 1 tablespoon dill, chopped

Directions:
4. Heat up a pot with the oil over medium-high heat, add the onion and the celery, stir and sauté for 5 minutes.
5. Add the cauliflower and the rest of the ingredients, bring to a simmer and cook over medium heat for 35 minutes more.
6. Divide the soup into bowls and serve.

Nutrition: calories 135, fat 4, fiber 8, carbs 21.4, protein 7.7

Pork and Leeks Soup

Preparation time: 10 minutes
Cooking time: 40 minutes
Servings: 4

Ingredients:
- 1 pound pork stew meat, cubed
- Black pepper to the taste
- 5 leeks, chopped
- 1 yellow onion, chopped
- 2 tablespoons olive oil
- 1 tablespoon parsley, chopped
- 6 cups low-sodium beef stock

Directions:
4. Heat up a pot with the oil over medium-high heat, add the onion and the leeks, stir and sauté for 5 minutes.
5. Add the meat, stir and brown for 5 minutes more.
6. Add the rest of the ingredients, bring to a simmer and cook over medium heat for 30 minutes.
7. Ladle the soup into bowls and serve.

Nutrition: calories 395, fat 18.3, fiber 2.6, carbs 18.4, protein 38.2

Minty Shrimp and Broccoli Salad

Preparation time: 5 minutes
Cooking time: 20 minutes
Servings: 4

Ingredients:
- 1/3 cup low-sodium veggie stock
- 2 tablespoons olive oil
- 2 cups broccoli florets
- 1 pound shrimp, peeled and deveined
- Black pepper to the taste
- 1 yellow onion, chopped
- 4 cherry tomatoes, halved
- 2 garlic cloves, minced
- Juice of ½ lemon
- ½ cup kalamata olives, pitted and cut into halves
- 1 tablespoon mint, chopped

Directions:
1. Heat up a pan with the oil over medium-high heat, add the onion and the garlic, stir and sauté for 3 minutes.
2. Add the shrimp, toss and cook for 2 minutes more.
3. Add the broccoli and the other ingredients, toss, cook everything for 10 minutes, divide into bowls and serve for lunch.

Nutrition: calories 270, fat 11.3, fiber 4.1, carbs 14.3, protein 28.9

Shrimp and Cod Soup

Preparation time: 10 minutes
Cooking time: 20 minutes
Servings: 4

Ingredients:
- 1 quart low-sodium chicken stock
- ½ pound shrimp, peeled and deveined
- ½ pound cod fillets, boneless, skinless and cubed
- 2 tablespoons olive oil
- 2 teaspoons chili powder
- 1 teaspoon sweet paprika
- 2 shallots, chopped
- A pinch of black pepper
- 1 tablespoon dill, chopped

Directions:
1. Heat up a pot with the oil over medium heat, add the shallots, stir and sauté for 5 minutes.
2. Add the shrimp and the cod, and cook for 5 minutes more.
3. Add the rest of the ingredients, bring to a simmer and cook over medium heat for 10 minutes.
4. Divide the soup into bowls and serve.

Nutrition: calories 189, fat 8.8, fiber 0.8, carbs 3.2, protein 24.6

Shrimp and Green Onions Mix

Preparation time: 10 minutes
Cooking time: 10 minutes
Servings: 4

Ingredients:
- 2 pounds shrimp, peeled and deveined
- 1 cup cherry tomatoes, halved
- 1 tablespoon olive oil
- 4 green onion, chopped
- 1 tablespoon balsamic vinegar
- 1 tablespoon chives, chopped

Directions:
1. Heat up a pan with the oil over medium heat, add the onion, and the cherry tomatoes, stir and sauté for 4 minutes.
2. Add the shrimp and the other ingredients, cook for 6 minutes more, divide between plates and serve.

Nutrition: calories 313, fat 7.5, fiber 1, carbs 6.4, protein 52.4

Spinach Stew

Preparation time: 10 minutes
Cooking time: 15 minutes
Servings: 4

Ingredients:
- 1 tablespoons olive oil
- 1 teaspoon ginger, grated
- 2 garlic cloves, minced
- 1 yellow onion, chopped
- 2 tomatoes, chopped
- 1 cup canned tomatoes, no-salt-added
- 1 teaspoon cumin, ground
- A pinch of black pepper
- 1 cup low-sodium veggie stock
- 2 pounds spinach leaves

Directions:
1. Heat up a pot with the oil over medium heat, add the ginger, garlic and the onion, stir and sauté for 5 minutes.
2. Add the tomatoes, canned tomatoes and the other ingredients, toss gently, bring to a simmer and cook for 10 minutes more.
3. Divide the stew into bowls and serve.

Nutrition: calories 123, fat 4.8, fiber 7.3, carbs 17, protein 8.2

Curry Cauliflower Mix

Preparation time: 10 minutes
Cooking time: 25 minutes
Servings: 4

Ingredients:
- 1 red onion, chopped
- 1 tablespoon olive oil
- 2 garlic cloves, minced
- 1 red bell pepper, chopped
- 1 green bell pepper, chopped
- 1 tablespoon lime juice
- 1 pound cauliflower florets
- 14 ounces canned tomatoes, chopped
- 2 teaspoons curry powder
- A pinch of black pepper
- 2 cups coconut cream
- 1 tablespoon cilantro, chopped

Directions:
1. Heat up a pot with the oil over medium heat, add the onion and the garlic, stir and cook for 5 minutes.
2. Add the bell peppers and the other ingredients, bring everything to a simmer and cook over medium heat for 20 minutes.
3. Divide everything into bowls and serve.

Nutrition: calories 270, fat 7.7, fiber 5.4, carbs 12.9, protein 7

Carrots and Zucchini Stew

Preparation time: 10 minutes
Cooking time: 30 minutes
Servings: 4

Ingredients:
- 1 yellow onion, chopped
- 2 tablespoons olive oil
- 2 garlic cloves, minced
- 4 zucchinis, sliced
- 2 carrots, sliced
- 1 teaspoon sweet paprika
- ¼ teaspoon chili powder
- A pinch of black pepper
- ½ cup tomatoes, chopped
- 2 cups low-sodium veggie stock
- 1 tablespoon chives, chopped
- 1 tablespoon rosemary, chopped

Directions:
1. Heat up a pot with the oil over medium heat, add the onion and the garlic, stir and sauté for 5 minutes.
2. Add the zucchinis, carrots and the other ingredients, bring to a simmer and cook for 25 minutes more.
3. Divide the stew in to bowls and serve right away for lunch.

Nutrition: calories 272, fat 4.6, fiber 4.7, carbs 14.9, protein 9

Cabbage and Green Beans Stew

Preparation time: 10 minutes
Cooking time: 25 minutes
Servings: 4

Ingredients:
- 2 tablespoons olive oil
- 1 red cabbage head, shredded
- 1 red onion, chopped
- 1 pound green beans, trimmed and halved
- 2 garlic cloves, minced
- 7 ounces canned tomatoes, no-salt-added chopped
- 2 cups low-sodium veggie stock
- A pinch of black pepper
- 1 tablespoon dill, chopped

Directions:
1. Heat up a pot with the oil, over medium heat, add the onion and the garlic, stir and sauté for 5 minutes.
2. Add the cabbage and the other ingredients, stir, cover and simmer over medium heat for 20 minutes.
3. Divide into bowls and serve for lunch.

Nutrition: calories 281, fat 8.5, fiber 7.1, carbs 14.9, protein 6.7

Chili Mushroom Soup

Preparation time: 5 minutes
Cooking time: 30 minutes
Servings: 4

Ingredients:
- 1 yellow onion, chopped
- 1 tablespoon olive oil
- 1 red chili pepper, chopped
- 1 teaspoon chili powder
- ½ teaspoon hot paprika
- 4 garlic cloves, minced
- 1 pound white mushrooms, sliced
- 6 cups low-sodium veggie stock
- 1 cup tomatoes, chopped
- ½ tablespoon parsley, chopped

Directions:
1. Heat up a pot with the oil, over medium heat, add the onion, chili pepper, hot paprika, chili powder and the garlic, stir and sauté for 5 minutes.
2. Add the mushrooms, stir and cook for 5 minutes more.
3. Add the rest of the ingredients, bring to a simmer and cook over medium heat for 20 minutes.
4. Divide the soup into bowls and serve.

Nutrition: calories 290, fat 6.6, fiber 4.6, carbs 16.9, protein 10

Chili Pork

Preparation time: 10 minutes
Cooking time: 30 minutes
Servings: 4

Ingredients:
- 2 pounds pork stew meat, cubed
- 2 tablespoons chili paste
- 1 yellow onion, chopped
- 2 garlic cloves, minced
- 1 tablespoon olive oil
- 2 cups low-sodium beef stock
- 1 tablespoon oregano, chopped

Directions:
1. Heat up a pot with the oil, over medium-high heat, add the onion and the garlic, stir and sauté for 5 minutes.
2. Add the meat and brown it for 5 minutes more.
3. Add the rest of the ingredients, bring to a simmer and cook over medium heat for 20 minutes more.
4. Divide the mix into bowls and serve.

Nutrition: calories 363, fat 8.6, fiber 7, carbs 17.3, protein 18.4

Paprika Mushroom and Salmon Salad

Preparation time: 10 minutes
Cooking time: 20 minutes
Servings: 4

Ingredients:
- 10 ounces smoked salmon, low-sodium, boneless, skinless and cubed
- 2 green onions, chopped
- 2 red chili peppers, chopped
- 1 tablespoon olive oil
- ½ teaspoon oregano, dried
- ½ teaspoon smoked paprika
- A pinch of black pepper
- 8 ounces white mushrooms, sliced
- 1 tablespoon lemon juice
- 1 cup black olives, pitted and halved
- 1 tablespoon parsley, chopped

Directions:
1. Heat up a pan with the oil over medium heat, add the onions and chili peppers, stir and cook for 4 minutes.
2. Add the mushrooms, stir and sauté them for 5 minutes.
3. Add the salmon and the other ingredients, toss, cook everything for 10 minutes more, divide into bowls and serve for lunch.

Nutrition: calories 321, fat 8.5, fiber 8, carbs 22.2, protein 13.5

Chickpeas and Potatoes Medley

Preparation time: 10 minutes
Cooking time: 30 minutes
Servings: 4

Ingredients:
- 2 tablespoons olive oil
- 1 cup canned chickpeas, no-salt-added, drained and rinsed
- 1 pound sweet potatoes, peeled and cut into wedges
- 4 garlic cloves, minced
- 2 shallots, chopped
- 1 cup canned tomatoes, no-salt-added and chopped
- 1 teaspoon coriander, ground
- 2 tomatoes, chopped
- 1 cup low-sodium veggie stock
- A pinch of black pepper
- 1 tablespoon lemon juice
- 1 tablespoon cilantro, chopped

Directions:
1. Heat up a pot with the oil over medium heat, add the shallots and the garlic, stir and sauté for 5 minutes.
2. Add the chickpeas, potatoes and the other ingredients, bring to a simmer and cook over medium heat for 25 minutes.
3. Divide everything into bowls and serve for lunch.

Nutrition: calories 341, fat 11.7, fiber 6, carbs 14.9, protein 18.7

Cardamom Chicken Mix

Preparation time: 10 minutes
Cooking time: 30 minutes
Servings: 4

Ingredients:
- 1 tablespoon olive oil
- 1 pound chicken breast, skinless, boneless and cubed
- 1 shallot, chopped
- 1 tablespoon ginger, grated
- 2 garlic cloves, minced
- 1 teaspoon cardamom, ground
- ½ teaspoon turmeric powder
- 1 teaspoon lime juice
- 1 cup low-sodium chicken stock
- 1 tablespoon cilantro, chopped

Directions:
1. Heat up a pot with the oil over medium-high heat, add the shallot, ginger, garlic, cardamom and the turmeric, stir and sauté for 5 minutes.
2. Add the meat and brown it for 5 minutes.
3. Add the rest of the ingredients, bring everything to a simmer and cook for 20 minutes.
4. Divide the mix into bowls and serve.

Nutrition: calories 175, fat 6.5, fiber 0.5, carbs 3.3, protein 24.7

Lentils Chili

Preparation time: 10 minutes
Cooking time: 35 minutes
Servings: 6

Ingredients:
- 1 green bell pepper, chopped
- 1 tablespoon olive oil
- 2 spring onions, chopped
- 2 garlic cloves, minced
- 24 ounces canned lentils, no-salt-added, drained and rinsed
- 2 cups veggie stock
- 2 tablespoons chili powder, mild
- ½ teaspoon chipotle powder
- 30 ounces canned tomatoes, no-salt-added, chopped
- A pinch of black pepper

Directions:
1. Heat up a pot with the oil over medium heat, add the onions and the garlic, stir and sauté for 5 minutes.
2. Add the bell pepper, lentils and the other ingredients, bring to a simmer and cook over medium heat for 30 minutes.
3. Divide the chili into bowls and serve for lunch.

Nutrition: calories 466, fat 5, fiber 37.6, carbs 77.9, protein 31.2

Rosemary Endives

Preparation time: 10 minutes
Cooking time: 20 minutes
Servings: 4

Ingredients:
- 2 endives, halved lengthwise
- 2 tablespoons olive oil
- 1 teaspoon rosemary, dried
- ½ teaspoon turmeric powder
- A pinch of black pepper

Directions:
1. In a baking pan, combine the endives with the oil and the other ingredients, toss gently, introduce in the oven and bake at 400 degrees F for 20 minutes.
2. Divide between plates and serve as a side dish.

Nutrition: calories 66, fat 7.1, fiber 1, carbs 1.2, protein 0.3

Lemony Endives

Preparation time: 10 minutes
Cooking time: 20 minutes
Servings: 4

Ingredients:
- 4 endives, halved lengthwise
- 1 tablespoon lemon juice
- 1 tablespoon lemon zest, grated
- 2 tablespoons fat-free parmesan, grated
- 2 tablespoons olive oil
- A pinch of black pepper

Directions:
1. In a baking dish, combine the endives with the lemon juice and the other ingredients except the parmesan and toss.
2. Sprinkle the parmesan on top, bake the endives at 400 degrees F for 20 minutes, divide between plates and serve as a side dish.

Nutrition: calories 71, fat 7.1, fiber 0.9, carbs 2.3, protein 0.9

Pesto Asparagus

Preparation time: 10 minutes
Cooking time: 20 minutes
Servings: 4

Ingredients:
- 1 pound asparagus, trimmed
- 2 tablespoons basil pesto
- 1 tablespoon lemon juice
- A pinch of black pepper
- 3 tablespoons olive oil
- 2 tablespoons cilantro, chopped

Directions:
1. Arrange the asparagus n a lined baking sheet, add the pesto and the other ingredients, toss, introduce in the oven and cook at 400 degrees F for 20 minutes.
2. Divide between plates and serve as a side dish.

Nutrition: calories 114, fat 10.7, fiber 2.4, carbs 4.6, protein 2.6

Paprika Carrots

Preparation time: 10 minutes
Cooking time: 30 minutes
Servings: 4

Ingredients:
- 1 pound baby carrots, trimmed
- 1 tablespoon sweet paprika
- 1 teaspoon lime juice
- 3 tablespoons olive oil
- A pinch of black pepper
- 1 teaspoon sesame seeds

Directions:
1. Arrange the carrots on a lined baking sheet, add the paprika and the other ingredients except the sesame seeds, toss, introduce in the oven and bake at 400 degrees F for 30 minutes.
2. Divide the carrots between plates, sprinkle sesame seeds on top and serve as a side dish.

Nutrition: calories 142, fat 11.3, fiber 4.1, carbs 11.4, protein 1.2

Creamy Potato Pan

Preparation time: 10 minutes
Cooking time: 1 hour
Servings: 8

Ingredients:
- 1 pound gold potatoes, peeled and cut into wedges
- 2 tablespoons olive oil
- 1 red onion, chopped
- 2 garlic cloves, minced
- 2 cups coconut cream
- 1 tablespoon thyme, chopped
- ¼ teaspoon nutmeg, ground
- ½ cup low-fat parmesan, grated

Directions:
1. Heat up a pan with the oil over medium heat, add the onion and the garlic and sauté for 5 minutes.
2. Add the potatoes and brown them for 5 minutes more.
3. Add the cream and the rest of the ingredients, toss gently, bring to a simmer and cook over medium heat for 40 minutes more.
4. Divide the mix between plates and serve as a side dish.

Nutrition: calories 230, fat 19.1, fiber 3.3, carbs 14.3, protein 3.6

Sesame Cabbage

Preparation time: 10 minutes
Cooking time: 20 minutes
Servings: 4

Ingredients:
- 1 pound green cabbage, roughly shredded
- 2 tablespoons olive oil
- A pinch of black pepper
- 1 shallot, chopped
- 2 garlic cloves, minced
- 2 tablespoons balsamic vinegar
- 2 teaspoons hot paprika
- 1 teaspoon sesame seeds

Directions:
1. Heat up a pan with the oil over medium heat, add the shallot and the garlic and sauté for 5 minutes.
2. Add the cabbage and the other ingredients, toss, cook over medium heat for 15 minutes, divide between plates and serve.

Nutrition: calories 101, fat 7.6, fiber 3.4, carbs 84, protein 1.9

Cilantro Broccoli

Preparation time: 10 minutes
Cooking time: 30 minutes
Servings: 4

Ingredients:
- 2 tablespoons olive oil
- 1 pound broccoli florets
- 2 garlic cloves, minced
- 2 tablespoons chili sauce
- 1 tablespoon lemon juice
- A pinch of black pepper
- 2 tablespoons cilantro, chopped

Directions:
1. In a baking pan, combine the broccoli with the oil, garlic and the other ingredients, toss a bit, introduce in the oven and bake at 400 degrees F for 30 minutes.
2. Divide the mix between plates and serve as a side dish.

Nutrition: calories 103, fat 7.4, fiber 3, carbs 8.3, protein 3.4

Chili Brussels Sprouts

Preparation time: 10 minutes
Cooking time: 25 minutes
Servings: 4

Ingredients:
- 1 tablespoon olive oil
- 1 pound Brussels sprouts, trimmed and halved
- 2 garlic cloves, minced
- ½ cup low-fat mozzarella, shredded
- A pinch of pepper flakes, crushed

Directions:
1. In a baking dish, combine the sprouts with the oil and the other ingredients except the cheese and toss.
2. Sprinkle the cheese on top, introduce in the oven and bake at 400 degrees F for 25 minutes.
3. Divide between plates and serve as a side dish.

Nutrition: calories 91, fat 4.5, fiber 4.3, carbs 10.9, protein 5

Brussels Sprouts and Green Onions Mix

Preparation time: 10 minutes
Cooking time: 25 minutes
Servings: 4

Ingredients:
- 2 tablespoons olive oil
- 1 pound Brussels sprouts, trimmed and halved
- 3 green onions, chopped
- 2 garlic cloves, minced
- 1 tablespoon balsamic vinegar
- 1 tablespoon sweet paprika
- A pinch of black pepper

Directions:
1. In a baking pan, combine the Brussels sprouts with the oil and the other ingredients, toss and bake at 400 degrees F for 25 minutes.
2. Divide the mix between plates and serve.

Nutrition: calories 121, fat 7.6, fiber 5.2, carbs 12.7, protein 4.4

Mashed Cauliflower

Preparation time: 10 minutes
Cooking time: 25 minutes
Servings: 4

Ingredients:
- 2 pounds cauliflower florets
- ½ cup coconut milk
- A pinch of black pepper
- ½ cup low-fat sour cream
- 1 tablespoon cilantro, chopped
- 1 tablespoon chives, chopped

Directions:
1. Put the cauliflower in a pot, add water to cover, bring to a boil over medium heat, cook for 25 minutes and drain.
2. Mash the cauliflower, add the milk, black pepper and the cream, whisk well, divide between plates, sprinkle the rest of the ingredients on top and serve.

Nutrition: calories 188, fat 13.4, fiber 6.4, carbs 15, protein 6.1

Avocado Salad

Preparation time: 5 minutes
Cooking time: 0 minutes
Servings: 4

Ingredients:
- 2 tablespoons olive oil
- 2 avocados, peeled, pitted and cut into wedges
- 1 cup kalamata olives, pitted and halved
- 1 cup tomatoes, cubed
- 1 tablespoon ginger, grated
- A pinch of black pepper
- 2 cups baby arugula
- 1 tablespoon balsamic vinegar

Directions:
1. In a bowl, combine the avocados with the kalamata and the other ingredients, toss and serve as a side dish.

Nutrition: calories 320, fat 30.4, fiber 8.7, carbs 13.9, protein 3

Radish Salad

Preparation time: 5 minutes
Cooking time: 0 minutes
Servings: 4

Ingredients:
- 2 green onions, sliced
- 1 pound radishes, cubed
- 2 tablespoons balsamic vinegar
- 2 tablespoon olive oil
- 1 teaspoon chili powder
- 1 cup black olives, pitted and halved
- A pinch of black pepper

Directions:
1. In a large salad bowl, combine radishes with the onions and the other ingredients, toss and serve as a side dish.

Nutrition: calories 123, fat 10.8, fiber 3.3, carbs 7, protein 1.3

Lemony Endives Salad

Preparation time: 5 minutes
Cooking time: 0 minutes
Servings: 4

Ingredients:
- 2 endives, roughly shredded
- 1 tablespoon dill, chopped
- ¼ cup lemon juice
- ¼ cup olive oil
- 2 cups baby spinach
- 2 tomatoes, cubed
- 1 cucumber, sliced
- ½ cups walnuts, chopped

Directions:
1. In a large bowl, combine the endives with the spinach and the other ingredients, toss and serve as a side dish.

Nutrition: calories 238, fat 22.3, fiber 3.1, carbs 8.4, protein 5.7

Olives and Corn Mix

Preparation time: 5 minutes
Cooking time: 0 minutes
Servings: 4

Ingredients:
- 2 tablespoons olive oil
- 1 tablespoon balsamic vinegar
- A pinch of black pepper
- 4 cups corn
- 2 cups black olives, pitted and halved
- 1 red onion, chopped
- ½ cup cherry tomatoes, halved
- 1 tablespoon basil, chopped
- 1 tablespoon jalapeno, chopped
- 2 cups romaine lettuce, shredded

Directions:
1. In a large bowl, combine the corn with the olives, lettuce and the other ingredients, toss well, divide between plates and serve as a side dish.

Nutrition: calories 290, fat 16.1, fiber 7.4, carbs 37.6, protein 6.2

Arugula and Pine Nuts Salad

Preparation time: 5 minutes
Cooking time: 0 minutes
Servings: 4

Ingredients:
- ¼ cup pomegranate seeds
- 5 cups baby arugula
- 6 tablespoons green onions, chopped
- 1 tablespoon balsamic vinegar
- 2 tablespoons olive oil
- 3 tablespoons pine nuts
- ½ shallot, chopped

Directions:
1. In a salad bowl, combine the arugula with the pomegranate and the other ingredients, toss and serve.

Nutrition: calories 120, fat 11.6, fiber 0.9, carbs 4.2, protein 1.8

Almonds and Spinach

Preparation time: 10 minutes
Cooking time: 0 minutes
Servings: 4

Ingredients:
- 2 tablespoons olive oil
- 2 avocados, peeled, pitted and cut into wedges
- 3 cups baby spinach
- ¼ cup almonds, toasted and chopped
- 1 tablespoon lemon juice
- 1 tablespoon cilantro, chopped

Directions:
1. In a bowl, combine the avocados with the almonds, spinach and the other ingredients, toss and serve as a side dish.

Nutrition: calories 181, fat 4, fiber 4.8, carbs 11.4, protein 6

Green Beans and Corn Salad

Preparation time: 4 minutes
Cooking time: 0 minutes
Servings: 4

Ingredients:
- Juice of 1 lime
- 2 cups romaine lettuce, shredded
- 1 cup corn
- ½ pound green beans, blanched and halved
- 1 cucumber, chopped
- 1/3 cup chives, chopped

Directions:
1. In a bowl, combine the green beans with the corn and the other ingredients, toss and serve.

Nutrition: calories 225, fat 12, fiber 2.4, carbs 11.2, protein 3.5

Endives and Kale Salad

Preparation time: 4 minutes
Cooking time: 0 minutes
Servings: 4

Ingredients:
- 3 tablespoons olive oil
- 2 endives, trimmed and shredded
- 2 tablespoons lime juice
- 1 tablespoon lime zest, grated
- 1 red onion, sliced
- 1 tablespoon balsamic vinegar
- 1 pound kale, torn
- A pinch of black pepper

Directions:
1. In a bowl, combine the endives with the kale and the other ingredients, toss well and serve cold as a side salad.

Nutrition: calories 270, fat 11.4, fiber 5, carbs 14.3, protein 5.7

Edamame Salad

Preparation time: 5 minutes
Cooking time: 6 minutes
Servings: 4

Ingredients:
- 2 tablespoons olive oil
- 2 tablespoons balsamic vinegar
- 2 garlic cloves, minced
- 3 cups edamame, shelled
- 1 tablespoon chives, chopped
- 2 shallots, chopped

Directions:
1. Heat up a pan with the oil over medium heat, add the edamame, the garlic and the other ingredients, toss, cook for 6 minutes, divide between plates and serve.

Nutrition: calories 270, fat 8.4, fiber 5.3, carbs 11.4, protein 6

Grapes and Avocados Salad

Preparation time: 5 minutes
Cooking time: 0 minutes
Servings: 4

Ingredients:
- 2 cups baby spinach
- 2 avocados, peeled, pitted and roughly cubed
- 1 cucumber, sliced
- 1 and ½ cups green grapes, halved
- 2 tablespoons avocado oil
- 1 tablespoon cider vinegar
- 2 tablespoons parsley, chopped
- A pinch of black pepper

Directions:
1. In a salad bowl, combine the baby spinach with the avocados and the other ingredients, toss and serve.

Nutrition: calories 277, fat 11.4, fiber 5, carbs 14.6, protein 4

Oregano Eggplant Mix

Preparation time: 10 minutes
Cooking time: 20 minutes
Servings: 4

Ingredients:
- 2 big eggplants, roughly cubed
- 1 tablespoon oregano, chopped
- ½ cup low-fat parmesan, grated
- ¼ teaspoon garlic powder
- 2 tablespoons olive oil
- A pinch of black pepper

Directions:
1. In a baking pan combine the eggplants with the oregano and the other ingredients except the cheese and toss.
2. Sprinkle parmesan on top, introduce in the oven and bake at 370 degrees F for 20 minutes.
3. Divide between plates and serve as a side dish.

Nutrition: calories 248, fat 8.4, fiber 4, carbs 14.3, protein 5.4

Baked Tomatoes Mix

Preparation time: 10 minutes
Cooking time: 20 minutes
Servings: 4

Ingredients:
- 2 pounds tomatoes, halved
- 1 tablespoon basil, chopped
- 3 tablespoons olive oil
- Zest of 1 lemon, grated
- 3 garlic cloves, minced
- ¼ cup low-fat parmesan, grated
- A pinch of black pepper

Directions:
1. In a baking pan, combine the tomatoes with the basil and the other ingredients except the cheese and toss.
2. Sprinkle the parmesan on top, introduce in the oven at 375 degrees F for 20 minutes, divide between plates and serve as a side dish.

Nutrition: calories 224, fat 12, fiber 4.3, carbs 10.8, protein 5.1

Thyme Mushrooms

Preparation time: 10 minutes
Cooking time: 30 minutes
Servings: 4

Ingredients:
- 2 pounds white mushrooms, halved
- 4 garlic cloves, minced
- 2 tablespoons olive oil
- 1 tablespoon thyme, chopped
- 2 tablespoons parsley, chopped
- Black pepper to the taste

Directions:
1. In a baking pan, combine the mushrooms with the garlic and the other ingredients, toss, introduce in the oven and cook at 400 degrees F for 30 minutes.
2. Divide between plates and serve as a side dish.

Nutrition: calories 251, fat 9.3, fiber 4, carbs 13.2, protein 6

Spinach and Corn Sauté

Preparation time: 10 minutes
Cooking time: 15 minutes
Servings: 4

Ingredients:
- 1 cup corn
- 1 pound spinach leaves
- 1 teaspoon sweet paprika
- 1 tablespoon olive oil
- 1 yellow onion, chopped
- ½ cup basil, torn
- A pinch of black pepper
- ½ teaspoon red pepper flakes

Directions:
1. Heat up a pan with the oil over medium-high heat, add the onion, stir and sauté for 5 minutes.
2. Add the corn, spinach and the other ingredients, toss, cook over medium heat for 10 minutes more, divide between plates and serve.

Nutrition: calories 201, fat 13.1, fiber 2.5, carbs 14.4, protein 3.7

Corn and Scallions Sauté

Preparation time: 10 minutes
Cooking time: 15 minutes
Servings: 4

Ingredients:
- 4 cups corn
- 1 tablespoon avocado oil
- 2 shallots, chopped
- 1 teaspoon chili powder
- 2 tablespoons tomato paste, no-salt-added
- 3 scallions, chopped
- A pinch of black pepper

Directions:
1. Heat up a pan with the oil over medium-high heat, add the scallions and chili powder, stir and sauté for 5 minutes.
2. Add the corn and the other ingredients, toss, cook for 10 minutes more, divide between plates and serve as a side dish.

Nutrition: calories 259, fat 11.1, fiber 2.6, carbs 13.2, protein 3.5

Spinach and Mango Salad

Preparation time: 10 minutes
Cooking time: 0 minutes
Servings: 4

Ingredients:
- 1 cup mango, peeled and cubed
- 4 cups baby spinach
- 1 tablespoon olive oil
- 2 spring onions, chopped
- 1 tablespoon lemon juice
- 1 tablespoon capers, drained, no-salt-added
- 1/3 cup almonds, chopped

Directions:
1. In a bowl, mix the spinach with the mango an d the other ingredients, toss and serve.

Nutrition: calories 200, fat 7.4, fiber 3, carbs 4.7, protein 4.4

Mustard Potatoes

Preparation time: 5 minutes
Cooking time: 1 hour
Servings: 4

Ingredients:
- 1 pound gold potatoes, peeled and cut into wedges
- 2 tablespoons olive oil
- A pinch of black pepper
- 2 tablespoons rosemary, chopped
- 1 tablespoon Dijon mustard
- 2 garlic cloves, minced

Directions:
1. In a baking pan, combine the potatoes with the oil and the other ingredients, toss, introduce in the oven at 400 degrees F and bake for about 1 hour.
2. Divide between plates and serve as a side dish right away.

Nutrition: calories 237, fat 11.5, fiber 6.4, carbs 14.2, protein 9

Coconut Brussels Sprouts

Preparation time: 5 minutes
Cooking time: 30 minutes
Servings: 4

Ingredients:
- 1 pound Brussels sprouts, trimmed and halved
- 1 cup coconut cream
- 1 tablespoon olive oil
- 2 shallots, chopped
- A pinch of black pepper
- ½ cup cashews, chopped

Directions:
1. In a roasting pan, combine the sprouts with the cream and the rest of the ingredients, toss, and bake in the oven for 30 minutes at 350 degrees F.
2. Divide between plates and serve as a side dish.

Nutrition: calories 270, fat 6.5, fiber 5.3, carbs 15.9, protein 3.4

Sage Carrots

Preparation time: 10 minutes
Cooking time: 30 minutes
Servings: 4

Ingredients:
- 2 tablespoons olive oil
- 2 teaspoons sweet paprika
- 1 pound carrots, peeled and roughly cubed
- 1 red onion, chopped
- 1 tablespoon sage, chopped
- A pinch of black pepper

Directions:
1. In a baking pan, combine the carrots with the oil and the other ingredients, toss and bake at 380 degrees F for 30 minutes.
2. Divide between plates and serve.

Nutrition: calories 200, fat 8.7, fiber 2.5, carbs 7.9, protein 4

Garlic Mushrooms and Corn

Preparation time: 10 minutes
Cooking time: 20 minutes
Servings: 4

Ingredients:
- 1 pound white mushrooms, halved
- 2 cups corn
- 2 tablespoons olive oil
- 4 garlic cloves, minced
- 1 cup canned tomatoes, no-salt-added, chopped
- A pinch of black pepper
- ½ teaspoon chili powder

Directions:
1. Heat up a pan with the oil over medium heat, add the mushrooms, garlic and the corn, stir and sauté for 10 minutes.
2. Add the rest of the ingredients, toss, cook over medium heat for 10 minutes more, divide between plates and serve.

Nutrition: calories 285, fat 13, fiber 2.2, carbs 14.6, protein 6.7.

Pesto Green Beans

Preparation time: 10 minutes
Cooking time: 15 minutes
Servings: 4

Ingredients:
- 2 tablespoons basil pesto
- 2 teaspoons sweet paprika
- 1 pound green beans, trimmed and halved
- Juice of 1 lemon
- 2 tablespoons olive oil
- 1 red onion, sliced
- A pinch of black pepper

Directions:
1. Heat up a pan with the oil over medium-high heat, add the onion, stir and sauté for 5 minutes.
2. Add the beans and the rest of the ingredients, toss, cook over medium heat fro 10 minutes, divide between plates and serve.

Nutrition: calories 280, fat 10, fiber 7.6, carbs 13.9, protein 4.7

Tarragon Tomatoes

Preparation time: 5 minutes
Cooking time: 0 minutes
Servings: 4

Ingredients:
- 1 and ½ tablespoon olive oil
- 1 pound tomatoes, cut into wedges
- 1 tablespoon lime juice
- 1 tablespoon lime zest, grated
- 2 tablespoons tarragon, chopped
- A pinch of black pepper

Directions:
1. In a bowl, combine the tomatoes with the other ingredients, toss and serve as a side salad.

Nutrition: calories 170, fat 4, fiber 2.1, carbs 11.8, proteins 6

Almond Beets

Preparation time: 10 minutes
Cooking time: 30 minutes
Servings: 4

Ingredients:
- 4 beets, peeled and cut into wedges
- 3 tablespoons olive oil
- 2 tablespoons almonds, chopped
- 2 tablespoons balsamic vinegar
- A pinch of black pepper
- 2 tablespoons parsley, chopped

Directions:
1. In a baking pan, combine the beets with the oil and the other ingredients, toss, introduce in the oven and bake at 400 degrees f for 30 minutes.
2. Divide the mix between plates and serve.

Nutrition: calories 230, fat 11, fiber 4.2, carbs 7.3, protein 3.6

Minty Tomatoes and Corn

Preparation time: 5 minutes
Cooking time: 0 minutes
Servings: 4

Ingredients:
- 2 tablespoons mint, chopped
- 1 pound tomatoes, cut into wedges
- 2 cups corn
- 2 tablespoons olive oil
- 1 tablespoon rosemary vinegar
- A pinch of black pepper

Directions:
1. In a salad bowl, combine the tomatoes with the corn and the other ingredients, toss and serve.

Enjoy!

Nutrition: calories 230, fat 7.2, fiber 2, carbs 11.6, protein 4

Zucchini and Avocado Salsa

Preparation time: 5 minutes
Cooking time: 10 minutes
Servings: 4

Ingredients:
- 2 tablespoons olive oil
- 2 zucchinis, cubed
- 1 avocado, peeled, pitted and cubed
- 2 tomatoes, cubed
- 1 cucumber, cubed
- 1 yellow onion, chopped
- 2 tablespoons fresh lime juice
- 2 tablespoons cilantro, chopped

Directions:
1. Heat up a pan with the oil over medium heat, add the onion and the zucchinis, toss and cook for 5 minutes.
2. Add the rest of the ingredients, toss, cook for 5 minutes more, divide between plates and serve.

Nutrition: calories 290, fat 11.2, fiber 6.1, carbs 14.7, protein 5.6

Apples and Cabbage Mix

Preparation time: 5 minutes
Cooking time: 0 minutes
Servings: 4

Ingredients:
- 2 green apples, cored and cubed
- 1 red cabbage head, shredded
- 2 tablespoons balsamic vinegar
- ½ teaspoon caraway seeds
- 2 tablespoons olive oil
- Black pepper to the taste

Directions:
1. In a bowl, combine the cabbage with the apples and the other ingredients, toss and serve as a side salad.

Nutrition: calories 165, fat 7.4, fiber 7.3, carbs 26, protein 2.6

Roasted Beets

Preparation time: 10 minutes
Cooking time: 30 minutes
Servings: 4

Ingredients:
- 4 beets, peeled and cut into wedges
- 2 tablespoons olive oil
- 2 garlic cloves, minced
- A pinch of black pepper
- ¼ cup parsley, chopped
- ¼ cup walnuts, chopped

Directions:
1. In a baking dish, combine the beets with the oil and the other ingredients, toss to coat, introduce in the oven at 420 degrees F, bake for 30 minutes, divide between plates and serve as a side dish.

Nutrition: calories 156, fat 11.8, fiber 2.7, carbs 11.5, protein 3.8

Dill Cabbage

Preparation time: 10 minutes
Cooking time: 15 minutes
Servings: 4

Ingredients:
- 1 pound green cabbage, shredded
- 1 yellow onion, chopped
- 1 tomato, cubed
- 1 tablespoon dill, chopped
- A pinch of black pepper
- 1 tablespoon olive oil

Directions:
1. Heat up a pan with the oil over medium heat, add the onion and sauté for 5 minutes.
2. Add the cabbage and the rest of the ingredients, toss, cook over medium heat for 10 minutes, divide between plates and serve.

Nutrition: calories 74, fat 3.7, fiber 3.7, carbs 10.2, protein 2.1

Cabbage and Carrot Salad

Preparation time: 5 minutes
Cooking time: 0 minutes
Servings: 4

Ingredients:
- 2 shallots, chopped
- 2 carrots, grated
- 1 big red cabbage head, shredded
- 1 tablespoon olive oil
- 1 tablespoon red vinegar
- A pinch of black pepper
- 1 tablespoon lime juice

Directions:
1. In a bowl, mix the cabbage with the shallots and the other ingredients, toss and serve as a side salad.

Nutrition: calories 106, fat 3.8, fiber 6.5, carbs 18, protein 3.3

Tomato and Olives Salsa

Preparation time: 10 minutes
Cooking time: 0 minutes
Servings: 6

Ingredients:
- 1 pound cherry tomatoes, halved
- 2 tablespoons olive oil
- 1 cup kalamata olives, pitted and halved
- A pinch of black pepper
- 1 red onion, chopped
- 1 tablespoon balsamic vinegar
- ¼ cup cilantro, chopped

Directions:
1. In a bowl, mix the tomatoes with the olives and the other ingredients, toss and serve as a side salad.

Nutrition: calories 131, fat 10.9, fiber 3.1, carbs 9.2, protein 1.6

Zucchini Salad

Preparation time: 4 minutes
Cooking time: 0 minutes
Servings: 4

Ingredients:
- 2 zucchinis, cut with a spiralizer
- 1 red onion, sliced
- 1 tablespoon basil pesto
- 1 tablespoon lemon juice
- 1 tablespoon olive oil
- ½ cup cilantro, chopped
- Black pepper to the taste

Directions:
1. In a salad bowl, mix the zucchinis with the onion and the other ingredients, toss and serve.

Nutrition: calories 58, fat 3.8, fiber 1.8, carbs 6, protein 1.6

Curry Carrots Slaw

Preparation time: 4 minutes
Cooking time: 0 minutes
Servings: 4

Ingredients:
- 1 pound carrots, peeled and roughly grated
- 2 tablespoons avocado oil
- 2 tablespoons lemon juice
- 3 tablespoons sesame seeds
- ½ teaspoon curry powder
- 1 teaspoon rosemary, dried
- ½ teaspoon cumin, ground

Directions:
1. In a bowl, mix the carrots with the oil, lemon juice and the other ingredients, toss and serve cold as a side salad.

Nutrition: calories 99, fat 4.4, fiber 4.2, carbs 13.7, protein 2.4

Lettuce and Beet Salad

Preparation time: 5 minutes
Cooking time: 0 minutes
Servings: 4

Ingredients:
- 1 tablespoon ginger, grated
- 2 garlic cloves, minced
- 4 cups romaine lettuce, torn
- 1 beet, peeled and grated
- 2 green onions, chopped
- 1 tablespoon balsamic vinegar
- 1 tablespoon sesame seeds

Directions:
1. In a bowl, combine the lettuce with the ginger, garlic and the other ingredients, toss and serve as a side dish.

Nutrition: calories 42, fat 1.4, fiber 1.5, carbs 6.7, protein 1.4

Herbed Radishes

Preparation time: 5 minutes
Cooking time: 0 minutes
Servings: 4

Ingredients:
- 1 pound red radishes, roughly cubed
- 1 tablespoon chives, chopped
- 1 tablespoon parsley, chopped
- 1 tablespoon oregano, chopped
- 2 tablespoons olive oil
- 1 tablespoon lime juice
- Black pepper to the taste

Directions:
1. In a salad bowl, mix the radishes with the chives and the other ingredients, toss and serve.

Nutrition: calories 85, fat 7.3, fiber 2.4, carbs 5.6, protein 1

Baked Fennel Mix

Preparation time: 5 minutes
Cooking time: 20 minutes
Servings: 4

Ingredients:
- 2 fennel bulbs, sliced
- 1 teaspoon sweet paprika
- 1 small red onion, sliced
- 2 tablespoons olive oil
- 2 tablespoons lime juice
- 2 tablespoons dill, chopped
- Black pepper to the taste

Directions:
1. In a roasting pan, combine the fennel with the paprika and the other ingredients, toss, and bake at 380 degrees F for 20 minutes.
2. Divide the mix between plates and serve.

Nutrition: calories 114, fat 7.4, fiber 4.5, carbs 13.2, protein 2.1

Roasted Peppers

Preparation time: 10 minutes
Cooking time: 30 minutes
Servings: 4

Ingredients:
- 1 pound mixed bell peppers, cut into wedges
- 1 red onion, thinly sliced
- 2 tablespoons olive oil
- Black pepper to the taste
- 1 tablespoon oregano, chopped
- 2 tablespoons mint leaves, chopped

Directions:
1. In a roasting pan, combine the bell peppers with the onion and the other ingredients, toss and bake at 380 degrees F for 30 minutes.
2. Divide the mix between plates and serve.

Nutrition: calories 240, fat 8.2, fiber 4.2, carbs 11.3, protein 5.6

Dates and Cabbage Sauté

Preparation time: 5 minutes
Cooking time: 15 minutes
Servings: 4

Ingredients:
- 1 pound red cabbage, shredded
- 8 dates, pitted and sliced
- 2 tablespoons olive oil
- ¼ cup low-sodium veggie stock
- 2 tablespoons chives, chopped
- 2 tablespoons lemon juice
- Black pepper to the taste

Directions:
1. Heat up a pan with the oil over medium heat, add the cabbage and the dates, toss and cook for 4 minutes.
2. Add the stock and the other ingredients, toss, cook over medium heat for 11 minutes more, divide between plates and serve.

Nutrition: calories 280, fat 8.1, fiber 4.1, carbs 8.7, protein 6.3

Black Beans Mix

Preparation time: 4 minutes
Cooking time: 0 minutes
Servings: 4

Ingredients:
- 3 cups canned black beans, no-salt-added, drained and rinsed
- 1 cup cherry tomatoes, halved
- 2 shallots, chopped
- 3 tablespoons olive oil
- 1 tablespoon balsamic vinegar
- Black pepper to the taste
- 1 tablespoon chives, chopped

Directions:
1. In a bowl, combine the beans with the tomatoes and the other ingredients, toss and serve cold as a side dish.

Nutrition: calories 310, fat 11.0, fiber 5.3, carbs 19.6, protein 6.8

Olives and Endives Mix

Preparation time: 4 minutes
Cooking time: 0 minutes
Servings: 4

Ingredients:
- 2 spring onions, chopped
- 2 endives, shredded
- 1 cup black olives, pitted and sliced
- ½ cup kalamata olives, pitted and sliced
- ¼ cup apple cider vinegar
- 2 tablespoons olive oil
- 1 tablespoons cilantro, chopped

Directions:
1. In a bowl, mix the endives with the olives and the other ingredients, toss and serve.

Nutrition: calories 230, fat 9.1, fiber 6.3, carbs 14.6, protein 7.2

Tomatoes and Cucumber Salad

Preparation time: 5 minutes
Cooking time: 0 minutes
Servings: 4

Ingredients:
- ½ pound tomatoes, cubed
- 2 cucumber, sliced
- 1 tablespoon olive oil
- 2 spring onions, chopped
- Black pepper to the taste
- Juice of 1 lime
- ½ cup basil, chopped

Directions:
1. In a salad bowl, combine the tomatoes with the cucumber and the other ingredients, toss and serve cold.

Nutrition: calories 224, fat 11.2, fiber 5.1, carbs 8.9, protein 6.2

Peppers and Carrot Salad

Preparation time: 5 minutes
Cooking time: 0 minutes
Servings: 4

Ingredients:
- 1 cup cherry tomatoes, halved
- 1 yellow bell pepper, chopped
- 1 red bell pepper, chopped
- 1 green bell pepper, chopped
- ½ pound carrots, shredded
- 3 tablespoons red wine vinegar
- 2 tablespoons olive oil
- 1 tablespoon cilantro, chopped
- Black pepper to the taste

Directions:
1. In a salad bowl, mix the tomatoes with the peppers, carrots and the other ingredients, toss and serve as a side salad.

Nutrition: calories 123, fat 4, fiber 8.4, carbs 14.4, protein 1.1

Black Beans and Rice Mix

Preparation time: 10 minutes
Cooking time: 30 minutes
Servings: 4

Ingredients:
- 2 tablespoons olive oil
- 1 yellow onion, chopped
- 1 cup canned black beans, no-salt-added, drained and rinsed
- 2 cup black rice
- 4 cups low-sodium chicken stock
- 2 tablespoons thyme, chopped
- Zest of ½ lemon, grated
- A pinch of black pepper

Directions:
1. Heat up a pan with the oil over medium-high heat, add the onion, stir and sauté for 4 minutes.
2. Add the beans, rice and the other ingredients, toss, bring to a boil and cook over medium heat for 25 minutes.
3. Stir the mix, divide between plates and serve.

Nutrition: calories 290, fat 15.3, fiber 6.2, carbs 14.6, protein 8

Rice and Cauliflower Mix

Preparation time: 10 minutes
Cooking time: 25 minutes
Servings: 4

Ingredients:
- 1 cup cauliflower florets
- 1 cup white rice
- 2 cups low-sodium chicken stock
- 1 tablespoon avocado oil
- 2 shallots, chopped
- ¼ cup cranberries
- ½ cup almonds, sliced

Directions:
1. Heat up a pan with the oil over medium heat, add the shallots, stir and sauté for 5 minutes.
2. Add the cauliflower, the rice and the other ingredients, toss, bring to a simmer and cook over medium heat for 20 minutes.
3. Divide the mix between plates and serve.

Nutrition: calories 290, fat 15.1, fiber 5.6, carbs 7, protein 4.5

Balsamic Beans Mix

Preparation time: 10 minutes
Cooking time: 0 minutes
Servings: 4

Ingredients:
- 2 cups canned black beans, no-salt-added, drained and rinsed
- 2 cups canned white beans, no-salt-added, drained and rinsed
- 2 tablespoons balsamic vinegar
- 2 tablespoons olive oil
- 1 teaspoon oregano, dried
- 1 teaspoon basil, dried
- 1 tablespoon chives, chopped

Directions:
1. In a salad bowl, combine the beans with the vinegar and the other ingredients, toss and serve as a side salad.

Nutrition: calories 322, fat 15.1, fiber 10, carbs 22.0, protein 7

Creamy Beets

Preparation time: 5 minutes
Cooking time: 20 minutes
Servings: 4

Ingredients:
- 1 pound beets, peeled and cubed
- 1 red onion, chopped
- 1 tablespoon olive oil
- ½ cup coconut cream
- 4 tablespoons non-fat yogurt
- 1 tablespoon chives, chopped

Directions:
1. Heat up a pan with the oil over medium heat, add the onion, stir and sauté for 4 minutes.
2. Add the beets, cream and the other ingredients, toss, cook over medium heat for 15 minutes more, divide between plates and serve.

Nutrition: calories 250, fat 13.4, fiber 3, carbs 13.3, protein 6.4

Avocado and Bell Peppers Mix

Preparation time: 10 minutes
Cooking time: 14 minutes
Servings: 4

Ingredients:
- 1 tablespoon avocado oil
- 1 teaspoon sweet paprika
- 1 pound mixed bell peppers, cut into strips
- 1 avocado, peeled, pitted and halved
- 1 teaspoon garlic powder
- 1 teaspoon rosemary, dried
- ½ cup low-sodium veggie stock
- Black pepper to the taste

Directions:
1. Heat up a pan with the oil over medium-high heat, add all the bell peppers, stir and sauté for 5 minutes.
2. Add the rest of the ingredients, toss, cook for 9 minutes more over medium heat, divide between plates and serve.

Nutrition: calories 245, fat 13.8, fiber 5, carbs 22.5, protein 5.4

Roasted Sweet Potato and Beets

Preparation time: 10 minutes
Cooking time: 1 hour
Servings: 4

Ingredients:
- 3 tablespoons olive oil
- 2 sweet potatoes, peeled and cut into wedges
- 2 beets, peeled, and cut into wedges
- 1 tablespoon oregano, chopped
- 1 tablespoon lime juice
- Black pepper to the taste

Directions:
1. Arrange the sweet potatoes and the beets on a lined baking sheet, add the rest of the ingredients, toss, introduce in the oven and bake at 375 degrees F for 1 hour/
2. Divide between plates and serve as a side dish.

Nutrition: calories 240, fat 11.2, fiber 4, carbs 8.6, protein 12.1

Kale Sauté

Preparation time: 10 minutes
Cooking time: 15 minutes
Servings: 4

Ingredients:
- 2 tablespoons olive oil
- 3 tablespoons coconut aminos
- 1 pound kale, torn
- 1 red onion, chopped
- 2 garlic cloves, minced
- 1 tablespoon lime juice
- 1 tablespoon cilantro, chopped

Directions:
1. Heat up a pan with the olive oil over medium heat, add the onion and the garlic and sauté for 5 minutes.
2. Add the kale and the other ingredients, toss, cook over medium heat for 10 minutes, divide between plates and serve.

Nutrition: calories 200, fat 7.1, fiber 2, carbs 6.4, protein 6

Spiced Carrots

Preparation time: 10 minutes
Cooking time: 20 minutes
Servings: 4

Ingredients:
- 1 tablespoon lemon juice
- 1 tablespoon olive oil
- ½ teaspoon allspice, ground
- ½ teaspoon cumin, ground
- ½ teaspoon nutmeg, ground
- 1 pound baby carrots, trimmed
- 1 tablespoon rosemary, chopped
- Black pepper to the taste

Directions:
1. In a roasting pan, combine the carrots with the lemon juice, oil and the other ingredients, toss, introduce in the oven and bake at 400 degrees F for 20 minutes.
2. Divide between plates and serve.

Nutrition: calories 260, fat 11.2, fiber 4.5, carbs 8.3, protein 4.3

Lemony Artichokes

Preparation time: 10 minutes
Cooking time: 20 minutes
Servings: 4

Ingredients:
- 2 tablespoons lemon juice
- 4 artichokes, trimmed and halved
- 1 tablespoon dill, chopped
- 2 tablespoons olive oil
- A pinch of black pepper

Directions:
1. In a roasting pan, combine the artichokes with the lemon juice and the other ingredients, toss gently and bake at 400 degrees F for 20 minutes.
Divide between plates and serve.

Nutrition: calories 140, fat 7.3, fiber 8.9, carbs 17.7, protein 5.5

Broccoli, Beans and Rice

Preparation time: 10 minutes
Cooking time: 30 minutes
Servings: 4

Ingredients:
- 1 cup broccoli florets, chopped
- 1 cup canned black beans, no-salt-added, drained
- 1 cup white rice
- 2 cups low-sodium chicken stock
- 2 teaspoons sweet paprika
- Black pepper to the taste

Directions:
1. Put the stock in a pot, heat up over medium heat, add the rice and the other ingredients, toss, bring to a boil and cook for 30 minutes stirring from time to time.
2. Divide the mix between plates and serve as a side dish.

Nutrition: calories 347, fat 1.2, fiber 9, carbs 69.3, protein 15.1

Baked Squash Mix

Preparation time: 10 minutes
Cooking time: 45 minutes
Servings: 4

Ingredients:
- 2 tablespoons olive oil
- 2 pounds butternut squash, peeled, and cut into wedges
- 1 tablespoon lemon juice
- 1 teaspoon chili powder
- 1 teaspoon garlic powder
- 2 teaspoons cilantro, chopped
- A pinch of black pepper

Directions
1. In a roasting pan, combine the squash with the oil and the other ingredients, toss gently, bake in the oven at 400 degrees F for 45 minutes, divide between plates and serve as a side dish.

Nutrition: calories 167, fat 7.4, fiber 4.9, carbs 27.5, protein 2.5

Creamy Asparagus

Preparation time: 5 minutes
Cooking time: 20 minutes
Servings: 4

Ingredients:
- ½ teaspoon nutmeg, ground
- 1 pound asparagus, trimmed and halved
- 1 cup coconut cream
- 1 yellow onion, chopped
- 2 tablespoons olive oil
- 1 tablespoon lime juice
- 1 tablespoon cilantro, chopped

Directions:
1. Heat up a pan with the oil over medium heat, add the onion and the nutmeg, stir and sauté for 5 minutes.
2. Add the asparagus and the other ingredients, toss, bring to a simmer and cook over medium heat for 15 minutes.
3. Divide between plates and serve.

Nutrition: calories 236, fat 21.6, fiber 4.4, carbs 11.4, protein 4.2

Basil Turnips Mix

Preparation time: 10 minutes
Cooking time: 15 minutes
Servings: 4

Ingredients:
- 1 tablespoon avocado oil
- 4 turnips, sliced
- ¼ cup basil, chopped
- Black pepper to the taste
- ¼ cup low-sodium veggie stock
- ½ cup walnuts, chopped
- 2 garlic cloves, minced

Directions:
1. Heat up a pan with the oil over medium-high heat, add the garlic and the turnips and brown for 5 minutes.
2. Add the rest of the ingredients, toss, cook for 10 minutes more, divide between plates and serve.

Nutrition: calories 140, fat 9.7, fiber 3.3, carbs 10.5, protein 5

Rice and Capers Mix

Preparation time: 10 minutes
Cooking time: 20 minutes
Servings: 4

Ingredients:
- 1 cup white rice
- 1 tablespoon capers, chopped
- 2 cups low-sodium chicken stock
- 1 red onion, chopped
- 1 tablespoon avocado oil
- 1 tablespoon cilantro, chopped
- 1 teaspoon sweet paprika

Directions:
1. Heat up a pan with the oil over medium-high heat, add the onion, stir and sauté for 5 minutes.
2. Add the rice, capers and the other ingredients, toss, bring to a simmer and cook for 15 minutes.
3. Divide the mix between plates and serve as a side dish.

Nutrition: calories 189, fat 0.9, fiber 1.6, carbs 40.2, protein 4.3

Spinach and Kale Mix

Preparation time: 5 minutes
Cooking time: 15 minutes
Servings: 4

Ingredients:
- 2 cups baby spinach
- 5 cups kale, torn
- 2 shallots, chopped
- 2 garlic cloves, minced
- 1 cup canned tomatoes, no-salt-added, chopped
- 1 tablespoon olive oil

Directions:
1. Heat up a pan with the oil over medium-high heat, add the shallots, stir and sauté for 5 minutes.
2. Add the spinach, kale and the other ingredients, toss, cook for 10 minutes more, divide between plates and serve as a side dish.

Nutrition: calories 89, fat 3.7, fiber 2.2, carbs 12.4, protein 3.6

Shrimp and Pineapple mix

Preparation time: 10 minutes
Cooking time: 10 minutes
Servings: 4

Ingredients:
- 1 tablespoon olive oil
- 1 pound shrimp, peeled and deveined
- 1 cup pineapple, peeled and cubed
- Juice of 1 lemon
- A bunch of parsley, chopped

Directions:
1. Heat up a pan with the oil over medium heat, add the shrimp and cook for 3 minutes on each side.
2. Add the rest of the ingredients, cook everything for 4 minutes more, divide into bowls and serve.

Nutrition: calories 254, fat 13.3, fiber 6, carbs 14.9, protein 11

Salmon and Green Olives

Preparation time: 10 minutes
Cooking time: 20 minutes
Servings: 4

Ingredients:
- 1 yellow onion, chopped
- 1 cup green olives, pitted and halved
- 1 teaspoon chili powder
- Black pepper to the taste
- 2 tablespoons olive oil
- ¼ cup low-sodium veggie stock
- 4 salmon fillets, skinless and boneless
- 2 tablespoons chives, chopped

Directions:
1. Heat up a pan with the oil over medium-high heat, add the onion and sauté for 3 minutes.
2. Add the salmon and cook for 5 minutes on each side. Add the rest of the ingredients, cook the mix for 5 minutes more, divide between plates and serve.

Nutrition: calories 221, fat 12.1, fiber 5.4, carbs 8.5, protein 11.2

Salmon and Fennel

Preparation time: 5 minutes
Cooking time: 15 minutes
Servings: 4

Ingredients:
- 4 medium salmon fillets, skinless and boneless
- 1 fennel bulb, chopped
- ½ cup low-sodium veggie stock
- 2 tablespoons olive oil
- Black pepper to the taste
- ¼ cup low-sodium veggie stock
- 1 tablespoon lemon juice
- 1 tablespoon cilantro, chopped

Directions:
1. Heat up a pan with the oil over medium heat, add the fennel and cook for 3 minutes.
2. Add the fish and brown it for 4 minutes on each side.
3. Add the rest of the ingredients, cook everything for 4 minutes more, divide between plates and serve.

Nutrition: calories 252, fat 9.3, fiber 4.2, carbs 12.3, protein 9

Cod and Asparagus

Preparation time: 10 minutes
Cooking time: 14 minutes
Servings: 4

Ingredients:
- 1 tablespoon olive oil
- 1 red onion, chopped
- 1 pound cod fillets, boneless
- 1 bunch asparagus, trimmed
- Black pepper to the taste
- 1 cup coconut cream
- 1 tablespoon chives, chopped

Directions:
1. Heat up a pan with the oil over medium heat, add the onion and the cod and cook it for 3 minutes on each side.
2. Add the rest of the ingredients, cook everything for 8 minutes more, divide between plates and serve.

Nutrition: calories 254, fat 12.1, fiber 5.4, carbs 4.2, protein 13.5

Spiced Shrimp

Preparation time: 5 minutes
Cooking time: 8 minutes
Servings: 4

Ingredients:
- 1 teaspoon garlic powder
- 1 teaspoon smoked paprika
- 1 teaspoon cumin, ground
- 1 teaspoon allspice, ground
- 2 tablespoons olive oil
- 2 pounds shrimp, peeled and deveined
- 1 tablespoon chives, chopped

Directions:
1. Heat up a pan with the oil over medium heat, add the shrimp, garlic powder and the other ingredients, cook for 4 minutes on each side, divide into bowls and serve.

Nutrition: calories 212, fat 9.6, fiber 5.3, carbs 12.7, protein 15.4

Sea Bass and Tomatoes

Preparation time: 10 minutes
Cooking time: 30 minutes
Servings: 4

Ingredients:
- 2 tablespoons olive oil
- 2 pounds sea bass fillets, skinless and boneless
- Black pepper to the taste
- 2 cups cherry tomatoes, halved
- 1 tablespoon chives, chopped
- 1 tablespoon lemon zest, grated
- ¼ cup lemon juice

Directions:
1. Grease a roasting pan with the oil and arrange the fish inside.
2. Add the tomatoes and the other ingredients, introduce the pan in the oven and bake at 380 degrees F for 30 minutes.
3. Divide everything between plates and serve.

Nutrition: calories 272, fat 6.9, fiber 6.2, carbs 18.4, protein 9

Shrimp and Beans

Preparation time: 10 minutes
Cooking time: 12 minutes
Servings: 4

Ingredients:
- 1 pound shrimp, deveined and peeled
- 1 tablespoon olive oil
- Juice of 1 lime
- 1 cup canned black beans, no-salt-added, drained
- 1 shallot, chopped
- 1 tablespoon oregano, chopped
- 2 garlic cloves, chopped
- Black pepper to the taste

Directions:
1. Heat up a pan with the oil over medium-high heat, add the shallot and the garlic, stir and cook for 3 minutes.
2. Add the shrimp and cook for 2 minutes on each side.
3. Add the beans and the other ingredients, cook everything over medium heat for 5 minutes more, divide into bowls and serve.

Nutrition: calories 253, fat 11.6, fiber 6, carbs 14.5, protein 13.5

Shrimp and Horseradish Mix

Preparation time: 5 minutes
Cooking time: 8 minutes
Servings: 4

Ingredients:
- 1 pound shrimp, peeled and deveined
- 2 shallots, chopped
- 1 tablespoon olive oil
- 1 tablespoon chives, chopped
- 2 teaspoons prepared horseradish
- ¼ cup coconut cream
- Black pepper to the taste

Directions:
4 Heat up a pan with the oil over medium heat, add the shallots and the horseradish, stir and sauté for 2 minutes.
5 Add the shrimp and the other ingredients, toss, cook for 6 minutes more, divide between plates and serve.

Nutrition: calories 233, fat 6, fiber 5, carbs 11.9, protein 5.4

Shrimp and Tarragon Salad

Preparation time: 4 minutes
Cooking time: 0 minutes
Servings: 4

Ingredients:
- 1 pound shrimp, cooked, peeled and deveined
- 1 tablespoon tarragon, chopped
- 1 tablespoon capers, drained
- 2 tablespoons olive oil
- Black pepper to the taste
- 2 cups baby spinach
- 1 tablespoon balsamic vinegar
- 1 small red onion, sliced
- 2 tablespoons lemon juice

Directions:
4 In a bowl, combine the shrimp with the tarragon and the other ingredients, toss and serve.

Nutrition: calories 258, fat 12.4, fiber 6, carbs 6.7, protein 13.3

Parmesan Cod Mix

Preparation time: 10 minutes
Cooking time: 20 minutes
Servings: 4

Ingredients:
- 4 cod fillets, boneless
- ½ cup low-fat parmesan cheese, shredded
- 3 garlic cloves, minced
- 1 tablespoon olive oil
- 1 tablespoon lemon juice
- ½ cup green onion, chopped

Directions:
1. Heat up a pan with the oil over medium heat, add the garlic and the green onions, toss and sauté for 5 minutes.
2. Add the fish and cook it for 4 minutes on each side.
3. Add the lemon juice, sprinkle the parmesan on top, cook everything for 2 minutes more, divide between plates and serve.

Nutrition: calories 275, fat 22.1, fiber 5, carbs 18.2, protein 12

Tilapia and Red Onion Mix

Preparation time: 10 minutes
Cooking time: 15 minutes
Servings: 4

Ingredients:
- 4 tilapia fillets, boneless
- 2 tablespoons olive oil
- 1 tablespoon lemon juice
- 2 teaspoons lemon zest, grated
- 2 red onions, roughly chopped
- 3 tablespoons chives, chopped

Directions:
1. Heat up a pan with the oil over medium heat, add the onions, lemon zest and lemon juice, toss and sauté for 5 minutes.
2. Add the fish and the chives, cook for 5 minutes on each side, divide between plates and serve.

Nutrition: calories 254, fat 18.2, fiber 5.4, carbs 11.7, protein 4.5

Trout Salad

Preparation time: 6 minutes
Cooking time: 0 minutes
Servings: 4

Ingredients:
- 4 ounces smoked trout, skinless, boneless and cubed
- 1 tablespoon lime juice
- 1/3 cup non-fat yogurt
- 2 avocados, peeled, pitted and cubed
- 3 tablespoons chives, chopped
- Black pepper to the taste
- 1 tablespoon olive oil

Directions:
1. In a bowl, combine the trout with the avocados and the other ingredients, toss, and serve.

Nutrition: calories 244, fat 9.45, fiber 5.6, carbs 8.5, protein 15

Balsamic Trout

Preparation time: 5 minutes
Cooking time: 15 minutes
Servings: 4

Ingredients:
- 3 tablespoons balsamic vinegar
- 2 tablespoons olive oil
- 4 trout fillets, boneless
- 3 tablespoons parsley, finely chopped
- 2 garlic cloves, minced

Directions:
1. Heat up a pan with the oil over medium heat, add the trout and cook for 6 minutes on each side.
2. Add the rest of the ingredients, cook for 3 minutes more, divide between plates and serve with a side salad.

Nutrition: calories 314, fat 14.3, fiber 8.2, carbs 14.8, protein 11.2

Parsley Salmon

Preparation time: 5 minutes
Cooking time: 12 minutes
Servings: 4

Ingredients:
- 2 spring onions, chopped
- 2 teaspoons lime juice
- 1 tablespoon chives, minced
- 1 tablespoon olive oil
- 4 salmon fillets, boneless
- Black pepper to the taste
- 2 tablespoons parsley, chopped

Directions:
1. Heat up a pan with the oil over medium heat, add the spring onions, stir and sauté for 2 minutes.
2. Add the salmon and the other ingredients, cook for 5 minutes on each side, divide between plates and serve.

Nutrition: calories 290, fat 14.4, fiber 5.6, carbs 15.6, protein 9.5

Trout and Veggie Salad

Preparation time: 5 minutes
Cooking time: 0 minutes
Servings: 4

Ingredients:
- 2 tablespoons olive oil
- ½ cup kalamata olives, pitted and minced
- Black pepper to the taste
- 1 pound smoked trout, boneless, skinless and cubed
- ½ teaspoon lemon zest, grated
- 1 tablespoon lemon juice
- 1 cup cherry tomatoes, halved
- ½ red onion, sliced
- 2 cups baby arugula

Directions:
1. In a bowl, combine smoked trout with the olives, black pepper and the other ingredients, toss and serve.

Nutrition: calories 282, fat 13.4, fiber 5.3, carbs 11.6, protein 5.6

Saffron Salmon

Preparation time: 10 minutes
Cooking time: 12 minutes
Servings: 4

Ingredients:
- Black pepper to the taste
- ½ teaspoon sweet paprika
- 4 salmon fillets, boneless
- 3 tablespoons olive oil
- 1 yellow onion, chopped
- 2 garlic cloves, minced
- ¼ teaspoon saffron powder

Directions:
1. Heat up a pan with the oil over medium-high heat, add the onion and the garlic, toss and sauté for 2 minutes.
2. Add the salmon and the other ingredients, cook for 5 minutes on each side, divide between plates and serve.

Nutrition: calories 339, fat 21.6, fiber 0.7, carbs 3.2, protein 35

Shrimp and Watermelon Salad

Preparation time: 10 minutes
Cooking time: 0 minutes
Servings: 4

Ingredients:
- ¼ cup basil, chopped
- 2 cups watermelon, peeled and cubed
- 2 tablespoons balsamic vinegar
- 2 tablespoons olive oil
- 1 pound shrimp, peeled, deveined and cooked
- Black pepper to the taste
- 1 tablespoon parsley, chopped

Directions:
1. In a bowl, combine the shrimp with the watermelon and the other ingredients, toss and serve.

Nutrition: calories 220, fat 9, fiber 0.4, carbs 7.6, protein 26.4

Oregano Shrimp and Quinoa Salad

Preparation time: 5 minutes
Cooking time: 8 minutes
Servings: 4

Ingredients:
- 1 pound shrimp, peeled and deveined
- 1 cup quinoa, cooked
- Black pepper to the taste
- 1 tablespoon olive oil
- 1 tablespoon oregano, chopped
- 1 red onion, chopped
- Juice of 1 lemon

Directions:
1. Heat up a pan with the oil over medium-high heat, add the onion, stir and sauté for 2 minutes.
2. Add the shrimp, toss and cook for 5 minutes.
3. Add the rest of the ingredients, toss, divide everything into bowls and serve.

Nutrition: calories 336, fat 8.2, fiber 4.1, carbs 32.3, protein 32.3

Crab Salad

Preparation time: 10 minutes
Cooking time: 0 minutes
Servings: 4

Ingredients:
- 1 tablespoon olive oil
- 2 cups crab meat
- Black pepper to the taste
- 1 cup cherry tomatoes, halved
- 1 shallot, chopped
- 1 tablespoon lemon juice
- 1/3 cup cilantro, chopped

Directions:
1. In a bowl, combine the crab with the tomatoes and the other ingredients, toss and serve.

Nutrition: calories 54, fat 3.9, fiber 0.6, carbs 2.6, protein 2.3

Balsamic Scallops

Preparation time: 4 minutes
Cooking time: 6 minutes
Servings: 4

Ingredients:
- 12 ounces sea scallops
- 2 tablespoons olive oil
- 2 garlic cloves, minced
- 1 tablespoon balsamic vinegar
- 1 cup scallions, sliced
- 2 tablespoons cilantro, chopped

Directions:
1. Heat up a pan with the oil over medium heat, add the scallions and the garlic and sauté for 2 minutes.
2. Add the scallops and the other ingredients, cook them for 2 minutes on each side, divide between plates and serve.

Nutrition: calories 146, fat 7.7, fiber 0.7, carbs 4.4, protein 14.8

Creamy Flounder Mix

Preparation time: 10 minutes
Cooking time: 20 minutes
Servings: 4

Ingredients:
- 2 tablespoon olive oil
- 1 red onion, chopped
- Black pepper to the taste
- ½ cup low-sodium veggie stock
- 4 flounder fillets, boneless
- ½ cup coconut cream
- 1 tablespoon dill, chopped

Directions:
1. Heat up a pan with the oil over medium heat, add the onion, stir and sauté for 5 minutes.
2. Add the fish and cook it for 4 minutes on each side.
3. Add the rest of the ingredients, cook for 7 minutes more, divide between plates and serve.

Nutrition: calories 232, fat 12.3, fiber 4, carbs 8.7, protein 12

Spicy Salmon and Mango Mix

Preparation time: 5 minutes
Cooking time: 0 minutes
Servings: 4

Ingredients:
- 1 pound smoked salmon, boneless, skinless and flaked
- Black pepper to the taste
- 1 red onion, chopped
- 1 mango, peeled, seedless and chopped
- 2 jalapeno peppers, chopped
- ¼ cup parsley, chopped
- 3 tablespoons lime juice
- 1 tablespoon olive oil

Directions:
2. In a bowl, mix the salmon with the black pepper and the other ingredients, toss and serve.

Nutrition: calories 323, fat 14.2, fiber 4, carbs 8.5, protein 20.4

Dill Shrimp Mix

Preparation time: 5 minutes
Cooking time: 0 minutes
Servings: 4

Ingredients:
- 2 teaspoons lemon juice
- 1 tablespoon olive oil
- 1 tablespoon dill, chopped
- 1 pound shrimp, cooked, peeled and deveined
- Black pepper to the taste
- 1 cup radishes, cubed

Directions:
1. In a bowl, combine the shrimp with the lemon juice and the other ingredients, toss and serve.

Nutrition: calories 292, fat 13, fiber 4.4, carbs 8, protein 16.4

Salmon Pate

Preparation time: 4 minutes
Cooking time: 0 minutes
Servings: 6

Ingredients:
- 6 ounces smoked salmon, boneless, skinless and shredded
- 2 tablespoons non-fat yogurt
- 3 teaspoons lemon juice
- 2 spring onions, chopped
- 8 ounces low-fat cream cheese
- ¼ cup cilantro, chopped

Directions:
1. In a bowl, mix the salmon with the yogurt and the other ingredients, whisk and serve cold.

Nutrition: calories 272, fat 15.2, fiber 4.3, carbs 16.8, protein 9.9

Shrimp with Artichokes

Preparation time: 4 minutes
Cooking time: 8 minutes
Servings: 4

Ingredients:
- 2 green onions, chopped
- 1 cup canned artichokes, no-salt-added, drained and quartered
- 2 tablespoons cilantro, chopped
- 1 pound shrimp, peeled and deveined
- 1 cup cherry tomatoes, cubed
- 1 tablespoon olive oil
- 1 tablespoon balsamic vinegar
- A pinch of salt and black pepper

Directions:
1. Heat up a pan with the oil over medium heat, add the onions and the artichokes, toss and cook for 2 minutes.
2. Add the shrimp, toss and cook over medium heat for 6 minutes.
3. Divide everything into bowls and serve.

Nutrition: calories 260, fat 8.23, fiber 3.8, carbs 14.3, protein 12.4

Shrimp with Lemon Sauce

Preparation time: 5 minutes
Cooking time: 8 minutes
Servings: 4

Ingredients:
- 1 pound shrimp, peeled and deveined
- 2 tablespoons olive oil
- Zest of 1 lemon, grated
- Juice of ½ lemon
- 1 tablespoon chives, chopped

Directions:
1. Heat up a pan with the oil over medium-high heat, add the lemon zest, lemon juice and the cilantro, toss and cook for 2 minutes.
2. Add the shrimp, cook everything for 6 minutes more, divide between plates and serve.

Nutrition: calories 195, fat 8.9, fiber 0, carbs 1.8, protein 25.9

Tuna and Orange Mix

Preparation time: 5 minutes
Cooking time: 12 minutes
Servings: 4

Ingredients:
- 4 tuna fillets, boneless
- Black pepper to the taste
- 2 tablespoons olive oil
- 2 shallots, chopped
- 3 tablespoons orange juice
- 1 orange, peeled and cut into segments
- 1 tablespoon oregano, chopped

Directions:
1. Heat up a pan with the oil over medium-high heat, add the shallots, stir and sauté for 2 minutes.
2. Add the tuna and the other ingredients, cook everything for 10 minutes more, divide between plates and serve.

Nutrition: calories 457, fat 38.2, fiber 1.6, carbs 8.2, protein 21.8

Salmon Curry

Preparation time: 10 minutes
Cooking time: 20 minutes
Servings: 4

Ingredients:
- 1 pound salmon fillet, boneless and cubed
- 3 tablespoons red curry paste
- 1 red onion, chopped
- 1 teaspoon sweet paprika
- 1 cup coconut cream
- 1 tablespoon olive oil
- Black pepper to the taste
- ½ cup low-sodium chicken stock
- 3 tablespoons basil, chopped

Directions:
1. Heat up a pan with the oil over medium-high heat, add the onion, paprika and the curry paste, toss and cook for 5 minutes.
2. Add the salmon and the other ingredients, toss gently, cook over medium heat for 15 minutes, divide into bowls and serve.

Nutrition: calories 377, fat 28.3, fiber 2.1, carbs 8.5, protein 23.9

Salmon and Carrots Mix

Preparation time: 10 minutes
Cooking time: 15 minutes
Servings: 4

Ingredients:
- 4 salmon fillets, boneless
- 1 red onion, chopped
- 2 carrots, sliced
- 2 tablespoons olive oil
- 2 tablespoons balsamic vinegar
- Black pepper to the taste
- 2 tablespoons chives, chopped
- ¼ cup low-sodium veggie stock

Directions:
1. Heat up a pan with the oil over medium heat, add the onion and the carrots, toss and sauté for 5 minutes.
2. Add the salmon and the other ingredients, cook everything for 10 minutes more, divide between plates and serve.

Nutrition: calories 322, fat 18, fiber 1.4, carbs 6, protein 35.2

Shrimp and Pine Nuts Mix

Preparation time: 10 minutes
Cooking time: 10 minutes
Servings: 4

Ingredients:
- 1 pound shrimp, peeled and deveined
- 2 tablespoons pine nuts
- 1 tablespoon lime juice
- 2 tablespoons olive oil
- 3 garlic cloves, minced
- Black pepper to the taste
- 1 tablespoon thyme, chopped
- 2 tablespoons chives, finely chopped

Directions:
1. Heat up a pan with the oil over medium-high heat, add the garlic, thyme, pine nuts and lime juice, toss and cook for 3 minutes.
2. Add the shrimp, black pepper and the chives, toss, cook for 7 minutes more, divide between plates and serve.

Nutrition: calories 290, fat 13, fiber 4.5, carbs 13.9, protein 10

Chili Cod and Green Beans

Preparation time: 10 minutes
Cooking time: 14 minutes
Servings: 4

Ingredients:
- 4 cod fillets, boneless
- ½ pound green beans, trimmed and halved
- 1 tablespoon lime juice
- 1 tablespoon lime zest, grated
- 1 yellow onion, chopped
- 2 tablespoons olive oil
- 1 teaspoon cumin, ground
- 1 teaspoon chili powder
- ½ cup low-sodium veggie stock
- A pinch of salt and black pepper

Directions:
1. Heat up a pan with the oil over medium-high heat, add the onion, toss and cook for 2 minutes.
2. Add the fish and cook it for 3 minutes on each side.
3. Add the green beans and the rest of the ingredients, toss gently, cook for 7 minutes more, divide between plates and serve.

Nutrition: calories 220, fat 13, carbs 14.3, fiber 2.3, protein 12

Garlic Scallops

Preparation time: 5 minutes
Cooking time: 8 minutes
Servings: 4

Ingredients:
- 12 scallops
- 1 red onion, sliced
- 2 tablespoons olive oil
- ½ teaspoon garlic, minced
- 2 tablespoons lemon juice
- Black pepper to the taste
- 1 teaspoon balsamic vinegar

Directions:
1. Heat up a pan with the oil over medium heat, add the onion and the garlic and sauté for 2 minutes.
2. Add the scallops and the other ingredients, cook over medium heat for 6 minutes more, divide between plates and serve hot.

Nutrition: calories 259, fat 8, fiber 3, carbs 5.7, protein 7

Creamy Sea Bass Mix

Preparation time: 10 minutes
Cooking time: 14 minutes
Servings: 4

Ingredients:
- 4 sea bass fillets, boneless
- 1 cup coconut cream
- 1 yellow onion, chopped
- 1 tablespoon lime juice
- 2 tablespoons avocado oil
- 1 tablespoon parsley, chopped
- A pinch of black pepper

Directions:
1. Heat up a pan with the oil over medium heat, add the onion, toss and sauté for 2 minutes.
2. Add the fish and cook it for 4 minutes on each side.
3. Add the rest of the ingredients, cook everything for 4 minutes more, divide between plates and serve.

Nutrition: calories 283, fat 12.3, fiber 5, carbs 12.5, protein 8

Sea Bass and Mushrooms Mix

Preparation time: 10 minutes
Cooking time: 13 minutes
Servings: 4

Ingredients:
- 4 sea bass fillets, boneless
- 2 tablespoons olive oil
- Black pepper to the taste
- ½ cup white mushrooms, sliced
- 1 red onion, chopped
- 2 tablespoons balsamic vinegar
- 3 tablespoons cilantro, chopped

Directions:
1. Heat up a pan with the oil over medium-high heat, add the onion and the mushrooms, stir and cook for 5 minutes.
2. Add the fish and the other ingredients, cook for 4 minutes on each side, divide everything between plates and serve.

Nutrition: calories 280, fat 12.3, fiber 8, carbs 13.6, protein 14.3

Salmon Chowder

Preparation time: 5 minutes
Cooking time: 20 minutes
Servings: 4

Ingredients:
- 1 pound salmon fillets, boneless, skinless and cubed
- 1 cup yellow onion, chopped
- 2 tablespoons olive oil
- Black pepper to the taste
- 2 cups low-sodium veggie stock
- 1 and ½ cups tomatoes, chopped
- 1 tablespoon basil, chopped

Directions:
1. Heat up a pot with the oil over medium heat, add the onion, stir and sauté for 5 minutes.
2. Add the salmon and the other ingredients, bring to a simmer and cook over medium heat for 15 minutes.
3. Divide the chowder into bowls and serve.

Nutrition: calories 250, fat 12.2, fiber 5, carbs 8.5, protein 7

Nutmeg Shrimp

Preparation time: 3 minutes
Cooking time: 6 minutes
Servings: 4

Ingredients:
- 1 pound shrimp, peeled and deveined
- 2 tablespoons olive oil
- 1 tablespoon lemon juice
- 1 tablespoon nutmeg, ground
- Black pepper to the taste
- 1 tablespoon cilantro, chopped

Directions:
1. Heat up a pan with the oil over medium heat, add the shrimp, lemon juice and the other ingredients, toss, cook for 6 minutes, divide into bowls and serve.

Nutrition: calories 205, fat 9.6, fiber 0.4, carbs 2.7, protein 26

Shrimp and Berries Mix

Preparation time: 4 minutes
Cooking time: 6 minutes
Servings: 4

Ingredients:
- 1 pound shrimp, peeled and deveined
- ½ cup tomatoes, cubed
- 2 tablespoons olive oil
- 1 tablespoon balsamic vinegar
- ½ cup strawberries, chopped
- Black pepper to the taste

Directions:
1. Heat up a pan with the oil over medium heat, add the shrimp, toss and cook for 3 minutes.
2. Add the rest of the ingredients, toss, cook for 3-4 minutes more, divide into bowls and serve.

Nutrition: calories 205, fat 9, fiber 0.6, carbs 4, protein 26.2

Baked Lemony Trout

Preparation time: 10 minutes
Cooking time: 30 minutes
Servings: 4

Ingredients:
- 4 trout
- 1 tablespoon lemon zest, grated
- 2 tablespoons olive oil
- 2 tablespoons lemon juice
- A pinch of black pepper
- 2 tablespoons cilantro, chopped

Directions:
1. In a baking dish, combine the fish with the lemon zest and the other ingredients and rub.
2. Bake at 370 degrees F for 30 minutes, divide between plates and serve.

Nutrition: calories 264, fat 12.3, fiber 5, carbs 7, protein 11

Chives Scallops

Preparation time: 3 minutes
Cooking time: 4 minutes
Servings: 4

Ingredients:
- 12 scallops
- 2 tablespoons olive oil
- Black pepper to the taste
- 2 tablespoons chives, chopped
- 1 tablespoon sweet paprika

Directions:
1. Heat up a pan with the oil over medium heat, add the scallops, paprika and the other ingredients, and cook for 2 minutes on each side.
2. Divide between plates and serve with a side salad.

Nutrition: calories 215, fat 6, fiber 5, carbs 4.5, protein 11

Tuna Meatballs

Preparation time: 10 minutes
Cooking time: 30 minutes
Servings: 4

Ingredients:
- 2 tablespoons olive oil
- 1 pound tuna, skinless, boneless and minced
- 1 yellow onion, chopped
- ¼ cup chives, chopped
- 1 egg, whisked
- 1 tablespoon coconut flour
- A pinch of salt and black pepper

Directions:
1. In a bowl, mix the tuna with the onion and the other ingredients except the oil, stir well and shape medium meatballs out of this mix.
2. Arrange the meatballs on a baking sheet, grease them with the oil, introduce in the oven at 350 degrees F, cook for 30 minutes, divide between plates and serve.

Nutrition: calories 291, fat 14.3, fiber 5, carbs 12.4, protein 11

Salmon Pan

Preparation time: 10 minutes
Cooking time: 12 minutes
Servings: 4

Ingredients:
- 4 salmon fillets, boneless and roughly cubed
- 2 tablespoons olive oil
- 1 red bell pepper, cut into strips
- 1 zucchini, roughly cubed
- 1 eggplant, roughly cubed
- 1 tablespoon lemon juice
- 1 tablespoon dill, chopped
- ¼ cup low-sodium veggie stock
- 1 teaspoon garlic powder
- A pinch of black pepper

Directions:
1. Heat up a pan with oil over medium-high heat, add the bell pepper, zucchini and the eggplant, toss and sauté for 3 minutes.
2. Add the salmon and the other ingredients, toss gently, cook everything for 9 minutes more, divide between plates and serve.

Nutrition: calories 348, fat 18.4, fiber 5.3, carbs 11.9, protein 36.9

Mustard Cod Mix

Preparation time: 10 minutes
Cooking time: 25 minutes
Servings: 4

Ingredients:
- 4 cod fillets, skinless and boneless
- A pinch of black pepper
- 1 teaspoon ginger, grated
- 1 tablespoon mustard
- 2 tablespoons olive oil
- 1 teaspoon thyme, dried
- ¼ teaspoon cumin, ground
- 1 teaspoon turmeric powder
- ¼ cup cilantro, chopped
- 1 cup low-sodium veggie stock
- 3 garlic cloves, minced

Directions:
1. In a roasting pan, combine the cod with the black pepper, ginger and the other ingredients, toss gently and bake at 380 degrees F for 25 minutes.
2. Divide the mix between plates and serve.

Nutrition: calories 176, fat 9, fiber 1, carbs 3.7, protein 21.2

Shrimp and Asparagus Mix

Preparation time: 10 minutes
Cooking time: 14 minutes
Servings: 4

Ingredients:
- 1 asparagus bunch, halved
- 1 pound shrimp, peeled and deveined
- Black pepper to the taste
- 2 tablespoons olive oil
- 1 red onion, chopped
- 2 garlic cloves, minced
- 1 cup coconut cream

Directions:
1. Heat up a pan with the oil over medium heat, add the onion, garlic and the asparagus, toss and cook for 4 minutes.
2. Add the shrimp and the other ingredients, toss, simmer over medium heat for 10 minutes, divide everything into bowls and serve.

Nutrition: calories 225, fat 6, fiber 3.4, carbs 8.6, protein 8

Cod and Peas

Preparation time: 10 minutes
Cooking time: 20 minutes
Servings: 4

Ingredients:
- 1 yellow onion, chopped
- 2 tablespoons olive oil
- ½ cup low-sodium chicken stock
- 4 cod fillets, boneless, skinless
- Black pepper to the taste
- 1 cup snow peas

Directions:
1. Heat up a pot with the oil over medium heat, add the onion, stir and sauté fro 4 minutes.
2. Add the fish and cook it for 3 minutes on each side.
3. Add the snow peas and the other ingredients, cook everything for 10 minutes more, divide between plates and serve.

Nutrition: calories 240, fat 8.4, fiber 2.7, carbs 7.6, protein 14

Shrimp and Mussels Bowls

Preparation time: 5 minutes
Cooking time: 12 minutes
Servings: 4

Ingredients:
- 1 pound mussels, scrubbed
- ½ cup low-sodium chicken stock
- 1 pound shrimp, peeled and deveined
- 2 shallots, minced
- 1 cup cherry tomatoes, cubed
- 2 garlic cloves, minced
- 1 tablespoon olive oil
- Juice of 1 lemon

Directions:
1. Heat up a pan with the oil over medium heat, add the shallots and the garlic and sauté for 2 minutes.
2. Add the shrimp, mussels and the other ingredients, cook everything over medium heat for 10 minutes, divide into bowls and serve.

Nutrition: calories 240, fat 4.9, fiber 2.4, carbs 11.6, protein 8

Dash Diet Dessert Recipes

Mint Cream

Preparation time: 2 hours and 4 minutes

Cooking time: 0 minutes
Servings: 4

Ingredients:
- 4 cups non-fat yogurt
- 1 cup coconut cream
- 3 tablespoons stevia
- 2 teaspoons lime zest, grated
- 1 tablespoon mint, chopped

Directions:
1. In a blender, combine the cream with the yogurt and the other ingredients, pulse well, divide into cups and keep in the fridge for 2 hours before serving.

Nutrition: calories 512, fat 14.3, fiber 1.5, carbs 83.6, protein 12.1

Raspberries Pudding

Preparation time: 10 minutes
Cooking time: 24 minutes
Servings: 4

Ingredients:
- 1 cup raspberries
- 2 teaspoons coconut sugar
- 3 eggs, whisked
- 1 tablespoon avocado oil
- ½ cup almond milk
- ½ cup coconut flour
- ¼ cup non-fat yogurt

Directions:
1. In a bowl, combine the raspberries with the sugar and the other ingredients except the cooking spray and whisk well.
2. Grease a pudding pan with the cooking spray, add the raspberries mix, spread, bake in the oven at 400 degrees F for 24 minutes, divide between dessert plates and serve.

Nutrition: calories 215, fat 11.3, fiber 3.4, carbs 21.3, protein 6.7

Almond Bars

Preparation time: 10 minutes
Cooking time: 30 minutes
Servings: 4

Ingredients:
- 1 cup almonds, crushed
- 2 eggs, whisked
- ½ cup almond milk
- 1 teaspoon vanilla extract
- 2/3 cup coconut sugar
- 2 cups whole flour
- 1 teaspoon baking powder
- Cooking spray

Directions:
1. In a bowl, combine the almonds with the eggs and the other ingredients except the cooking spray and stir well.
2. Pour this into a square pan greased with cooking spray, spread well, bake in the oven for 30 minutes, cool down, cut into bars and serve.

Nutrition: calories 463, fat 22.5, fiber 11, carbs 54.4, protein 16.9

Baked Peaches Mix

Preparation time: 10 minutes
Cooking time: 30 minutes
Servings: 4

Ingredients:
- 4 peaches, stones removed and halved
- 1 tablespoon coconut sugar
- 1 teaspoon vanilla extract
- ¼ teaspoon cinnamon powder
- 1 tablespoon avocado oil

Directions:
1. In a baking pan, combine the peaches with the sugar and the other ingredients, bake at 375 degrees F for 30 minutes, cool down and serve.

Nutrition: calories 91, fat 0.8, fiber 2.5, carb 19.2, protein 1.7

Walnuts Cake

Preparation time: 10 minutes
Cooking time: 25 minutes
Servings: 8

Ingredients:
- 3 cups almond flour
- 1 cup coconut sugar
- 1 tablespoon vanilla extract
- ½ cup walnuts, chopped
- 2 teaspoons baking soda
- 2 cups coconut milk
- ½ cup coconut oil, melted

Directions:
1. In a bowl, combine the almond flour with the sugar and the other ingredients, whisk well, pour into a cake pan, spread, introduce in the oven at 370 degrees F, bake for 25 minutes.
2. Leave the cake to cool down, slice and serve.

Nutrition: calories 445, fat 10, fiber 6.5, carbs 31.4, protein 23.5

Apple Cake

Preparation time: 10 minutes
Cooking time: 30 minutes
Servings: 4

Ingredients:
- 2 cups almond flour
- 1 teaspoon baking soda
- 1 teaspoon baking powder
- ½ teaspoon cinnamon powder
- 2 tablespoons coconut sugar
- 1 cup almond milk
- 2 green apples, cored, peeled and chopped
- Cooking spray

Directions:
1. In a bowl, combine the flour with the baking soda, the apples and the other ingredients except the cooking spray, and whisk well.
2. Pour this into a cake pan greased with the cooking spray, spread well, introduce in the oven and bake at 360 degrees F for 30 minutes.
3. Cool the cake down, slice and serve.

Nutrition: calories 332, fat 22.4, fiber 9l.6, carbs 22.2, protein 12.3

Cinnamon Cream

Preparation time: 2 hours
Cooking time: 10 minutes
Servings: 4

Ingredients:
- 1 cup non-fat almond milk
- 1 cup coconut cream
- 2 cups coconut sugar
- 2 tablespoons cinnamon powder
- 1 teaspoon vanilla extract

Directions:
1. Heat up a pan with the almond milk over medium heat, add the rest of the ingredients, whisk, and cook for 10 minutes more.
2. Divide the mix into bowls, cool down and keep in the fridge for 2 hours before serving.

Nutrition: calories 254, fat 7.5, fiber 5, carbs 16.4, protein 9.5

Creamy Strawberries Mix

Preparation time: 10 minutes
Cooking time: 0 minutes
Servings: 4

Ingredients:
- 1 teaspoon vanilla extract
- 2 cups strawberries, chopped
- 1 teaspoon coconut sugar
- 8 ounces non-fat yogurt

Directions:
1. In a bowl, combine the strawberries with the vanilla and the other ingredients, toss and serve cold.

Nutrition: calories 343, fat 13.4, fiber 6, carb 15.43, protein 5.5

Vanilla Pecan Brownies

Preparation time: 10 minutes
Cooking time: 25 minutes
Servings: 8

Ingredients:
- 1 cup pecans, chopped
- 3 tablespoons coconut sugar
- 2 tablespoons cocoa powder
- 3 eggs, whisked
- ¼ cup coconut oil, melted
- ½ teaspoon baking powder
- 2 teaspoons vanilla extract
- Cooking spray

Directions:
1. In your food processor, combine the pecans with the coconut sugar and the other ingredients except the cooking spray and pulse well.
2. Grease a square pan with cooking spray, add the brownies mix, spread, introduce in the oven, bake at 350 degrees F for 25 minutes, leave aside to cool down, slice and serve.

Nutrition: calories 370, fat 14.3, fiber 3, carbs 14.4, protein 5.6

Strawberries Cake

Preparation time: 10 minutes
Cooking time: 25 minutes
Servings: 6

Ingredients:
- 2 cups whole wheat flour
- 1 cup strawberries, chopped
- ½ teaspoon baking soda
- ½ cup coconut sugar
- ¾ cup coconut milk
- ¼ cup coconut oil, melted
- 2 eggs, whisked
- 1 teaspoon vanilla extract
- Cooking spray

Directions:
1. In a bowl, combine the flour with the strawberries and the other ingredients except the coking spray and whisk well.
2. Grease a cake pan with cooking spray, pour the cake mix, spread, bake in the oven at 350 degrees F for 25 minutes, cool down, slice and serve.

Nutrition: calories 465, fat 22.1, fiber 4, carbs 18.3, protein 13.4

Cocoa Pudding

Preparation time: 10 minutes
Cooking time: 10 minutes
Servings: 4

Ingredients:
- 2 tablespoons coconut sugar
- 3 tablespoons coconut flour
- 2 tablespoons cocoa powder
- 2 cups almond milk
- 2 eggs, whisked
- ½ teaspoon vanilla extract

Directions:
1. Put the milk in a pan, add the cocoa and the other ingredients, whisk, simmer over medium heat for 10 minutes, pour into small cups and serve cold.

Nutrition: calories 385, fat 31.7, fiber 5.7, carbs 21.6, protein 7.3

Nutmeg Vanilla Cream

Preparation time: 10 minutes
Cooking time: 0 minutes
Servings: 6

Ingredients:
- 3 cups non-fat milk
- 1 teaspoon nutmeg, ground
- 2 teaspoons vanilla extract
- 4 teaspoons coconut sugar
- 1 cup walnuts, chopped

Directions:
1. In a bowl, combine milk with the nutmeg and the other ingredients, whisk well, divide into small cups and serve cold.

Nutrition: calories 243, fat 12.4, fiber 1.5, carbs 21.1, protein 9.7

Avocado Cream

Preparation time: 1 hour and 10 minutes

Cooking time: 0 minutes
Servings: 4

Ingredients:
- 2 cups coconut cream
- 2 avocados, peeled, pitted and mashed
- 2 tablespoons coconut sugar
- 1 teaspoon vanilla extract

Directions:
1. In a blender, combine the cream with the avocados and the other ingredients, pulse well, divide into cups and keep in the fridge for 1 hour before serving.

Nutrition: calories 532, fat 48.2, fiber 9.4, carbs 24.9, protein 5.2

Raspberries Cream

Preparation time: 10 minutes
Cooking time: 25 minutes
Servings: 4

Ingredients:
- 2 tablespoons almond flour
- 1 cup coconut cream
- 3 cups raspberries
- 1 cup coconut sugar
- 8 ounces low-fat cream cheese

Directions:
1. In a bowl, the flour with the cream and the other ingredients, whisk, transfer to a round pan, cook at 360 degrees F for 25 minutes, divide into bowls and serve.

Nutrition: calories 429, fat 36.3, fiber 7.7, carbs 21.3, protein 7.8

Watermelon Salad

Preparation time: 4 minutes
Cooking time: 0 minutes
Servings: 4

Ingredients:
- 1 cup watermelon, peeled and cubed
- 2 apples, cored and cubed
- 1 tablespoon coconut cream
- 2 bananas, cut into chunks

Directions:
1. In a bowl, combine the watermelon with the apples and the other ingredients, toss and serve.

Nutrition: calories 131, fat 1.3, fiber 4.5, carbs 31.9, protein 1.3

Coconut Pears Mix

Preparation time: 10 minutes
Cooking time: 10 minutes
Servings: 4

Ingredients:
- 2 teaspoons lime juice
- ½ cup coconut cream
- ½ cup coconut, shredded
- 4 pears, cored and cubed
- 4 tablespoons coconut sugar

Directions:
1. In a pan, combine the pears with the lime juice and the other ingredients, stir, bring to a simmer over medium heat and cook for 10 minutes.
2. Divide into bowls and serve cold.

Nutrition: calories 320, fat 7.8, fiber 3, carbs 6.4, protein 4.7

Apples Compote

Preparation time: 10 minutes
Cooking time: 15 minutes
Servings: 4

Ingredients:
- 5 tablespoons coconut sugar
- 2 cups orange juice
- 4 apples, cored and cubed

Directions:
1. In a pot, combine apples with the sugar and the orange juice, toss, bring to a boil over medium heat, cook for 15 minutes, divide into bowls and serve cold.

Nutrition: calories 220, fat 5.2, fiber 3, carbs 5.6, protein 5.6

Apricots Stew

Preparation time: 10 minutes
Cooking time: 15 minutes
Servings: 4

Ingredients:
- 2 cups apricots, halved
- 2 cups water
- 2 tablespoons coconut sugar
- 2 tablespoons lemon juice

Directions:
1. In a pot, combine the apricots with the water and the other ingredients, toss, cook over medium heat for 15 minutes, divide into bowls and serve.

Nutrition: calories 260, fat 6.2, fiber 4.2, carbs 5.6, protein 6

Lemon Cantaloupe Mix

Preparation time: 10 minutes
Cooking time: 10 minutes
Servings: 4

Ingredients:
- 2 cups cantaloupe, peeled and roughly cubed
- 4 tablespoons coconut sugar
- 2 teaspoons vanilla extract
- 2 teaspoons lemon juice

Directions:
1. In a small pan, combine the cantaloupe with the sugar and the other ingredients, toss, heat up over medium heat, cook for about 10 minutes, divide into bowls and serve cold.

Nutrition: calories 140, fat 4, fiber 3.4, carbs 6.7, protein 5

Creamy Rhubarb Cream

Preparation time: 10 minutes
Cooking time: 14 minutes
Servings: 4

Ingredients:
- 1/3 cup low-fat cream cheese
- ½ cup coconut cream
- 2 pound rhubarb, roughly chopped
- 3 tablespoons coconut sugar

Directions:
1. In a blender, combine the cream cheese with the cream and the other ingredients and pulse well.
2. Divide into small cups, introduce in the oven and bake at 350 degrees F for 14 minutes.
3. Serve cold.

Nutrition: calories 360, fat 14.3, fiber 4.4, carbs 5.8, protein 5.2

Pineapple Bowls

Preparation time: 10 minuetes
Cooking time: 0 minutes
Servings: 4

Ingredients:
- 3 cups pineapple, peeled and cubed
- 1 teaspoon chia seeds
- 1 cup coconut cream
- 1 teaspoon vanilla extract
- 1 tablespoon mint, chopped

Directions:
1. In a bowl, combine the pineapple with the cream and the other ingredients, toss, divide into smaller bowls and keep in the fridge for 10 minutes before serving.

Nutrition: calories 238, fat 16.6, fiber 5.6, carbs 22.8, protein 3.3

Blueberry Stew

Preparation time: 10 minutes
Cooking time: 10 minutes
Servings: 4

Ingredients:
- 2 tablespoons lemon juice
- 1 cup water
- 3 tablespoons coconut sugar
- 12 ounces blueberries

Directions:
1. In a pan, combine the blueberries with the sugar and the other ingredients, bring to a gentle simmer and cook over medium heat for 10 minutes.
2. Divide into bowls and serve.

Nutrition: calories 122, fat 0.4, fiber 2.1, carbs 26.7, protein 1.5

Lime Pudding

Preparation time: 10 minutes
Cooking time: 15 minutes
Servings: 4

Ingredients:
- 2 cups coconut cream
- Juice of 1 lime
- Zest of 1 lime, grated
- 3 tablespoons coconut oil, melted
- 1 egg, whisked
- 1 teaspoon baking powder

Directions:
1. In a bowl, combine the cream with the lime juice and the other ingredients and whisk well.
2. Divide into small ramekins, introduce in the oven and bake at 360 degrees F for 15 minutes.
3. Serve the pudding cold.

Nutrition: calories 385, fat 39.9, fiber 2.7, carbs 8.2, protein 4.2

Peach Cream

Preparation time: 10 minutes
Cooking time: 0 minutes
Servings: 4

Ingredients:
- 3 cups coconut cream
- 2 peaches, stones removed and chopped
- 1 teaspoon vanilla extract
- ½ cup almonds, chopped

Directions:
1. In a blender, combine the cream and the other ingredients, pulse well, divide into small bowls and serve cold.

Nutrition: calories 261, fat 13, fiber 5.6, carbs 7, protein 5.4

Cinnamon Plums Mix

Preparation time: 10 minutes
Cooking time: 15 minutes
Servings: 4

Ingredients:
- 1 pound plums, stones removed and halved
- 2 tablespoons coconut sugar
- ½ teaspoon cinnamon powder
- 1 cup water

Directions:
1. In a pan, combine the plums with the sugar and the other ingredients, bring to a simmer and cook over medium heat for 15 minutes.
2. Divide into bowls and serve cold.

Nutrition: calories 142, fat 4, fiber 2.4, carbs 14, protein 7

Chia and Vanilla Apples

Preparation time: 10 minutes
Cooking time: 10 minutes
Servings: 4

Ingredients:
- 2 cups apples, cored and cut into wedges
- 2 tablespoons chia seeds
- 1 teaspoon vanilla extract
- 2 cups naturally unsweetened apple juice

Directions:
1. In a small pot, combine the apples with the chia seeds and the other ingredients, toss, cook over medium heat for 10 minutes, divide into bowls and serve cold.

Nutrition: calories 172, fat 5.6, fiber 3.5, carbs 10, protein 4.4

Rice and Pears Pudding

Preparation time: 10 minutes
Cooking time: 25 minutes
Servings: 4

Ingredients:
- 6 cups water
- 1 cup coconut sugar
- 2 cups black rice
- 2 pears, cored and cubed
- 2 teaspoons cinnamon powder

Directions:
1. Put the water in a pan, heat it up over medium-high heat, add the rice, sugar and the other ingredients, stir, bring to a simmer, reduce heat to medium and cook for 25 minutes.
2. Divide into bowls and serve cold.

Nutrition: calories 290, fat 13.4, fiber 4, carbs 13.20, protein 6.7

Rhubarb Stew

Preparation time: 10 minutes
Cooking time: 15 minutes
Servings: 4

Ingredients:
- 2 cups rhubarb, roughly chopped
- 3 tablespoons coconut sugar
- 1 teaspoon almond extract
- 2 cups water

Directions:
1. In a pot, combine the rhubarb with the other ingredients, toss, bring to a boil over medium heat, cook for 15 minutes, divide into bowls and serve cold.

Nutrition: calories 142, fat 4.1, fiber 4.2, carbs 7, protein 4

Rhubarb Cream

Preparation time: 1 hour
Cooking time: 10 minutes
Servings: 4

Ingredients:
- 2 cups coconut cream
- 1 cup rhubarb, chopped
- 3 eggs, whisked
- 3 tablespoons coconut sugar
- 1 tablespoon lime juice

Directions:
1. In a small pan, combine the cream with the rhubarb and the other ingredients, whisk well, simmer over medium heat for 10 minutes, blend using an immersion blender, divide into bowls and keep in the fridge for 1 hour before serving.

Nutrition: calories 230, fat 8.4, fiber 2.4, carbs 7.8, protein 6

Blueberries Salad

Preparation time: 5 minutes
Cooking time: 0 minutes
Servings: 4

Ingredients:
- 2 cups blueberries
- 3 tablespoons mint, chopped
- 1 pear, cored and cubed
- 1 apple, core and cubed
- 1 tablespoon coconut sugar

Directions:
1. In a bowl, combine the blueberries with the mint and the other ingredients, toss and serve cold.

Nutrition: calories 150, fat 2.4, fiber 4, carbs 6.8, protein 6

Dates and Banana Cream

Preparation time: 5 minutes
Cooking time: 0 minutes
Servings: 4

Ingredients:
- 1 cup almond milk
- 1 banana, peeled and sliced
- 1 teaspoon vanilla extract
- ½ cup coconut cream
- dates, chopped

Directions:
1. In a blender, combine the dates with the banana and the other ingredients, pulse well, divide into small cups and serve cold.

Nutrition: calories 271, fat 21.6, fiber 3.8, carbs 21.2, protein 2.7

Plum Muffins

Preparation time: 10 minutes
Cooking time: 25 minutes
Servings: 12

Ingredients:
- 3 tablespoons coconut oil, melted
- ½ cup almond milk
- 4 eggs, whisked
- 1 teaspoon vanilla extract
- 1 cup almond flour
- 2 teaspoons cinnamon powder
- ½ teaspoon baking powder
- 1 cup plums, pitted and chopped

Directions:
1. In a bowl, combine the coconut oil with the almond milk and the other ingredients and whisk well.
2. Divide into a muffin pan, introduce in the oven at 350 degrees F and bake for 25 minutes.
3. Serve the muffins cold.

Nutrition: calories 270, fat 3.4, fiber 4.4, carbs 12, protein 5

Plums and Raisins Bowls

Preparation time: 10 minutes
Cooking time: 20 minutes
Servings: 4

Ingredients:
- ½ pound plums, pitted and halved
- 2 tablespoons coconut sugar
- 4 tablespoons raisins
- 1 teaspoon vanilla extract
- 1 cup coconut cream

Directions:
1. In a pan, combine the plums with the sugar and the other ingredients, bring to a simmer and cook over medium heat for 20 minutes.
2. Divide into bowls and serve.

Nutrition: calories 219, fat 14.4, fiber 1.8, carbs 21.1, protein 2.2

Sunflower Seed Bars

Preparation time: 10 minutes
Cooking time: 20 minutes
Servings: 6

Ingredients:
- 1 cup coconut flour
- ½ teaspoon baking soda
- 1 tablespoon flax seed
- 3 tablespoons almond milk
- 1 cup sunflower seeds
- 2 tablespoons coconut oil, melted
- 1 teaspoon vanilla extract

Directions:
1. In a bowl, mix the flour with the baking soda and the other ingredients, stir really well, spread on a baking sheet, press well, bake in the oven at 350 degrees F for 20 minutes, leave aside to cool down, cut into bars and serve.

Nutrition: calories 189, fat 12.6, fiber 9.2, carbs 15.7, protein 4.7

Blackberries and Cashews Bowls

Preparation time: 10 minutes
Cooking time: 0 minutes
Servings: 4
Ingredients:

- 1 cup cashews
- 2 cups blackberries
- ¾ cup coconut cream
- 1 teaspoon vanilla extract
- 1 tablespoon coconut sugar

Directions:

1. In a bowl, combine the cashews with the berries and the other ingredients, toss, divide into small bowls and serve.

Nutrition: calories 230, fat 4, fiber 3.4, carbs 12.3, protein 8

Orange and Mandarins Bowls

Preparation time: 4 minutes
Cooking time: 8 minutes
Servings: 4

Ingredients:
- 4 oranges, peeled and cut into segments
- 2 mandarins, peeled and cut into segments
- Juice of 1 lime
- 2 tablespoons coconut sugar
- 1 cup water

Directions:
1. In a pan, combine the oranges with the mandarins and the other ingredients, bring to a simmer and cook over medium heat for 8 minutes.
2. Divide into bowls and serve cold.

Nutrition: calories 170, fat 2.3, fiber 2.3, carbs 11, protein 3.4

Pumpkin Cream

Preparation time: 2 hours
Cooking time: 0 minutes
Servings: 4

Ingredients:
- 2 cups coconut cream
- 1 cup pumpkin puree
- 14 ounces coconut cream
- 3 tablespoons coconut sugar

Directions:
1. In a bowl, combine the cream with the pumpkin puree and the other ingredients, whisk well, divide into small bowls and keep in the fridge for 2 hours before serving.

Nutrition: calories 350, fat 12.3, fiber 3, carbs 11.7, protein 6

Figs and Rhubarb Mix

Preparation time: 6 minutes
Cooking time: 14 minutes
Servings: 4

Ingredients:
- 2 tablespoons coconut oil, melted
- 1 cup rhubarb, roughly chopped
- 12 figs, halved
- ¼ cup coconut sugar
- 1 cup water

Directions:
1. Heat up a pan with the oil over medium heat, add the figs and the rest of the ingredients, toss, cook for 14 minutes, divide into small cups and serve cold.

Nutrition: calories 213, fat 7.4, fiber 6.1, carbs 39, protein 2.2

Spiced Banana

Preparation time: 4 minutes
Cooking time: 15 minutes
Servings: 4

Ingredients:
- 4 bananas, peeled and halved
- 1 teaspoon nutmeg, ground
- 1 teaspoon cinnamon powder
- Juice of 1 lime
- 4 tablespoons coconut sugar

Directions:
1. Arrange the bananas in a baking pan, add the nutmeg and the other ingredients, bake at 350 degrees F for 15 minutes.
2. Divide the baked bananas between plates and serve.

Nutrition: calories 206, fat 0.6, fiber 3.2, carbs 47.1, protein 2.4

Cocoa Smoothie

Preparation time: 5 minutes
Cooking time: 0 minutes
Servings: 2

Ingredients:

- 2 teaspoons cocoa powder
- 1 avocado, pitted, peeled and mashed
- 1 cup almond milk
- 1 cup coconut cream

Directions:

1. In your blender, combine the almond milk with the cream and the other ingredients, pulse well, divide in to cups and serve cold.

Nutrition: calories 155, fat 12.3, fiber 4, carbs 8.6, protein 5

Banana Bars

Preparation time: 30 minutes

Cooking time: 0 minutes

Servings: 4

Ingredients:

- 1 cup coconut oil, melted
- 2 bananas, peeled and chopped
- 1 avocado, peeled, pitted and mashed
- ½ cup coconut sugar
- ¼ cup lime juice
- 1 teaspoon lemon zest, grated
- Cooking spray

Directions:

1. In your food processor, mix the bananas with the oil and the other ingredients except the cooking spray and pulse well.
2. Grease a pan with the cooking spray, pour and spread the banana mix, spread, keep in the fridge for 30 minutes, cut into bars and serve.

Nutrition: calories 639, fat 64.6, fiber 4.9, carbs 20.5, protein 1.7

Green Tea and Dates Bars

Preparation time: 10 minutes
Cooking time: 30 minutes
Servings: 8

Ingredients:
- 2 tablespoons green tea powder
- 2 cups coconut milk, heated
- ½ cup coconut oil, melted
- 2 cups coconut sugar
- 4 eggs, whisked
- 2 teaspoons vanilla extract
- 3 cups almond flour
- 1 teaspoon baking soda
- 2 teaspoons baking powder

Directions:
1. In a bowl, combine the coconut milk with the green tea powder and the rest of the ingredients, stir well, pour into a square pan, spread, introduce in the oven, bake at 350 degrees F for 30 minutes, cool down, cut into bars and serve.

Nutrition: calories 560, fat 22.3, fiber 4, carbs 12.8, protein 22.1

Walnut Cream

Preparation time: 2 hours
Cooking time: 0 minutes
Servings: 4

Ingredients:
- 2 cups almond milk
- ½ cup coconut cream
- ½ cup walnuts, chopped
- 3 tablespoons coconut sugar
- 1 teaspoon vanilla extract

Directions:
1. In a bowl, combine the almond milk with the cream and the other ingredients, whisk well, divide into cups and keep in the fridge for 2 hours before serving.

Nutrition: calories 170, fat 12.4, fiber 3, carbs 12.8, protein 4

Lemon Cake

Preparation time: 10 minutes
Cooking time: 35 minutes
Servings: 6

Ingredients:
- 2 cups whole wheat flour
- 1 teaspoon baking powder
- 2 tablespoons coconut oil, melted
- 1 egg, whisked
- 3 tablespoons coconut sugar
- 1 cup almond milk
- Zest of 1 lemon, grated
- Juice of 1 lemon

Directions:
1. In a bowl, combine the flour with the oil and the other ingredients, whisk well, transfer this to a cake pan and bake at 360 degrees F for 35 minutes.
2. Slice and serve cold.

Nutrition: calories 222, fat 12.5, fiber 6.2, carbs 7, protein 17.4

Raisins Bars

Preparation time: 10 minutes
Cooking time: 25 minutes
Servings: 6

Ingredients:
- 1 teaspoon cinnamon powder
- 2 cups almond flour
- 1 teaspoon baking powder
- ½ teaspoon nutmeg, ground
- 1 cup coconut oil, melted
- 1 cup coconut sugar
- 1 egg, whisked
- 1 cup raisins

Directions:
1. In a bowl, combine the flour with the cinnamon and the other ingredients, stir well, spread on a lined baking sheet, introduce in the oven, bake at 380 degrees F for 25 minutes, cut into bars and serve cold.

Nutrition: calories 274, fat 12, fiber 5.2, carbs 14.5, protein 7

Nectarines Squares

Preparation time: 10 minutes
Cooking time: 20 minutes
Servings: 4

Ingredients:
- 3 nectarines, pitted and chopped
- 1 tablespoon coconut sugar
- ½ teaspoon baking soda
- 1 cup almond flour
- 4 tablespoons coconut oil, melted
- 2 tablespoons cocoa powder

Directions:
1. In a blender, combine the nectarines with the sugar and the rest of the ingredients, pulse well, pour into a lined square pan, spread, bake in the oven at 375 degrees F for 20 minutes, leave the mix aside to cool down a bit, cut into squares and serve.

Nutrition: calories 342, fat 14.4, fiber 7.6, carbs 12, protein 7.7

Grapes Stew

Preparation time: 10 minutes
Cooking time: 20 minutes
Servings: 4

Ingredients:
- 1 cup green grapes
- Juice of ½ lime
- 2 tablespoons coconut sugar
- 1 and ½ cups water
- 2 teaspoons cardamom powder

Directions:
1. Heat up a pan with the water medium heat, add the grapes and the other ingredients, bring to a simmer, cook for 20 minutes, divide into bowls and serve.

Nutrition: calories 384, fat 12.5, fiber 6.3, carbs 13.8, protein 5.6

Mandarin and Plums Cream

Preparation time: 10 minutes
Cooking time: 20 minutes
Servings: 4

Ingredients:
- 1 mandarin, peeled and chopped
- ½ pound plums, pitted and chopped
- 1 cup coconut cream
- Juice of 2 mandarins
- 2 tablespoons coconut sugar

Directions:
1. In a blender, combine the mandarin with the plums and the other ingredients, pulse well, divide into small ramekins, introduce in the oven, bake at 350 degrees F for 20 minutes, and serve cold.

Nutrition: calories 402, fat 18.2, fiber 2, carbs 22.2, protein 4.5

Cherry and Strawberries Cream

Preparation time: 10 minutes
Cooking time: 0 minutes
Servings: 6

Ingredients:
- 1 pound cherries, pitted
- 1 cup strawberries, chopped
- ¼ cup coconut sugar
- 2 cups coconut cream

Directions:
1. In a blender, combine the cherries with the other ingredients, pulse well, divide into bowls and serve cold.

Nutrition: calories 342, fat 22.1, fiber 5.6, carbs 8.4, protein 6.5

Cardamom Walnuts and Rice Pudding

Preparation time: 5 minutes
Cooking time: 40 minutes
Servings: 4

Ingredients:
- 1 cup basmati rice
- 3 cups almond milk
- 3 tablespoons coconut sugar
- ½ teaspoon cardamom powder
- ¼ cup walnuts, chopped

Directions:
1. In a pan, combine the rice with the milk and the other ingredients, stir, cook for 40 minutes over medium heat, divide into bowls and serve cold.

Nutrition: calories 703, fat 47.9, fiber 5.2, carbs 62.1, protein 10.1

Pears Bread

Preparation time: 10 minutes
Cooking time: 30 minutes
Servings: 4

Ingredients:
- 2 cups pears, cored and cubed
- 1 cup coconut sugar
- 2 eggs, whisked
- 2 cups almond flour
- 1 tablespoon baking powder
- 1 tablespoon coconut oil, melted

Directions:
1. In a bowl, mix the pears with the sugar and the other ingredients, whisk, pour into a loaf pan, introduce in the oven and bake at 350 degrees F for 30 minutes.
2. Slice and serve cold.

Nutrition: calories 380, fat 16.7, fiber 5, carbs 17.5, protein 5.6

Rice and Cherries Pudding

Preparation time: 10 minutes
Cooking time: 25 minutes
Servings: 4

Ingredients:
- 1 tablespoon coconut oil, melted
- 1 cup white rice
- 3 cups almond milk
- ½ cup cherries, pitted and halved
- 3 tablespoons coconut sugar
- 1 teaspoon cinnamon powder
- 1 teaspoon vanilla extract

Directions:
1. In a pan, combine the oil with the rice and the other ingredients, stir, bring to a simmer, cook for 25 minutes over medium heat, divide into bowls and serve cold.

Nutrition: calories 292, fat 12.4, fiber 5.6, carbs 8, protein 7

Watermelon Stew

Preparation time: 5 minutes
Cooking time: 8 minutes
Servings: 4

Ingredients:
- Juice of 1 lime
- 1 teaspoon lime zest, grated
- 1 and ½ cup coconut sugar
- 4 cups watermelon, peeled and cut into large chunks
- 1 and ½ cups water

Directions:
1. In a pan, combine the watermelon with the lime zest, and the other ingredients, toss, bring to a simmer over medium heat, cook for 8 minutes, divide into bowls and serve cold.

Nutrition:: calories 233, fat 0.2, fiber 0.7, carbs 61.5, protein 0.9

Ginger Pudding

Preparation time: 1 hour
Cooking time: 0 minutes
Servings: 4

Ingredients:
- 2 cups almond milk
- ½ cup coconut cream
- 2 tablespoons coconut sugar
- 1 tablespoon ginger, grated
- ¼ cup chia seeds

Directions:
1. In a bowl, combine the milk with the cream and the other ingredients, whisk well, divide into small cups and keep them in the fridge for 1 hour before serving.

Nutrition: calories 345, fat 17, fiber 4.7, carbs 11.5, protein 6.9

Cashew Cream

Preparation time: 2 hours
Cooking time: 0 minutes
Servings: 4

Ingredients:
- 1 cup cashews, chopped
- 2 tablespoons coconut oil, melted
- 2 tablespoons coconut oil, melted
- 1 cup coconut cream
- tablespoons lemon juice
- 1 tablespoons coconut sugar

Directions:
1. In a blender, combine the cashews with the coconut oil and the other ingredients, pulse well, divide into small cups and keep in the fridge for 2 hours before serving.

Nutrition: calories 480, fat 43.9, fiber 2.4, carbs 19.7, protein 7

Hemp Cookies

Preparation time: 30 minutes
Cooking time: 0 minutes
Servings: 6

Ingredients:
- 1 cup almonds, soaked overnight and drained
- 2 tablespoons cocoa powder
- 1 tablespoon coconut sugar
- ½ cup hemp seeds
- ¼ cup coconut, shredded
- ½ cup water

Directions:
1. In your food processor, combine the almonds with the cocoa powder and the other ingredients, pulse well, press this on a lined baking sheet, keep in the fridge for 30 minutes, slice and serve.

Nutrition: calories 270, fat 12.6, fiber 3, carbs 7.7, protein 7

Almonds and Pomegranate Bowls

Preparation time: 2 hours
Cooking time: 0 minutes
Servings: 4

Ingredients:
- ½ cup coconut cream
- 1 teaspoon vanilla extract
- 1 cup almonds, chopped
- 1 cup pomegranate seeds
- 1 tablespoon coconut sugar

Directions:
1. In a bowl, combine the almonds with the cream and the other ingredients, toss, divide into small bowls and serve.

Nutrition: calories 258, fat 19, fiber 3.9, carbs 17.6, protein 6.2

Chicken Thighs and Rosemary Veggies

Preparation time: 10 minutes
Cooking time: 40 minutes
Servings: 4

Ingredients:
- 2 pounds chicken breasts, skinless, boneless and cubed
- 1 carrot, cubed
- 1 celery stalk, chopped
- 1 tomato, cubed
- 2 small red onions, sliced
- 1 zucchini, cubed
- 2 garlic cloves, minced
- 1 tablespoon rosemary, chopped
- 2 tablespoons olive oil
- Black pepper to the taste
- ½ cup low-sodium veggie stock

Directions:
1. Heat up a pan with the oil over medium heat, add the onions and the garlic, stir and sauté for 5 minutes.
2. Add the chicken, toss and brown it for 5 minutes more.
3. Add the carrot and the other ingredients, toss, bring to a simmer and cook over medium heat for 30 minutes.
4. Divide the mix between plates and serve.

Nutrition: calories 325, fat 22.5, fiber 6.1, carbs 15.5, protein 33.2

Chicken with Carrots and Cabbage

Preparation time: 10 minutes
Cooking time: 25 minutes
Servings: 4

Ingredients:
- 1 pound chicken breast, skinless, boneless and cubed
- 2 tablespoons olive oil
- 2 carrots, peeled and grated
- 1 teaspoon sweet paprika
- ½ cup low-sodium veggie stock
- 1 red cabbage head, shredded
- 1 yellow onion, chopped
- Black pepper to the taste

Directions:
1. Heat up a pan with the oil over medium heat, add the onion, stir and sauté for 5 minutes.
2. Add the meat, and brown it for 5 minutes more.
3. Add the carrots and the other ingredients, toss, bring to a simmer and cook over medium heat for 15 minutes.
4. Divide everything between plates and serve.

Nutrition: calories 370, fat 22.2, fiber 5.2, carbs 44.2, protein 24.2

Eggplant and Turkey Sandwich

Preparation time: 10 minutes
Cooking time: 25 minutes
Servings: 4

Ingredients:
- 1 turkey breast, skinless, boneless and sliced into 4 pieces
- 1 eggplant, sliced into 4 slices
- Black pepper to the taste
- 1 tablespoon olive oil
- 1 tablespoon oregano, chopped
- ½ cup low sodium tomato sauce
- ½ cup low-fat cheddar cheese, shredded
- 4 whole wheat bread slices

Directions:
1. Heat up a grill over medium-high heat, add the turkey slices, drizzle half of the oil over them, sprinkle the black pepper, cook for 8 minutes on each side and transfer to a plate.
2. Arrange the eggplant slices on the heated grill, drizzle the rest of the oil over them, season with black pepper as well, cook them for 4 minutes on each side and transfer to the plate with the turkey slices as well.
3. Arrange 2 bread slices on a working surface, divide the cheese on each, divide the eggplant slices and turkey ones on each, sprinkle the oregano, drizzle the sauce all over and top with the other 2 bread slices.
4. Divide the sandwiches between plates and serve.

Nutrition: calories 280, fat 12.2, fiber 6, carbs 14, protein 12

Simple Turkey and Zucchini Tortillas

Preparation time: 10 minutes
Cooking time: 20 minutes
Servings: 4

Ingredients:
- 4 whole wheat tortillas
- ½ cup fat-free yogurt
- 1 pound turkey, breast, skinless, boneless and cut into strips
- 1 tablespoon olive oil
- 1 red onion, sliced
- 1 zucchini, cubed
- 2 tomatoes, cubed
- Black pepper to the taste

Directions:
1. Heat up a pan with the oil over medium heat, add the onion, stir and sauté for 5 minutes.
2. Add the zucchini and tomatoes, toss and cook for 2 minutes more.
3. Add the turkey meat, toss and cook for 13 minutes more.
4. Spread the yogurt on each tortilla, add divide the turkey and zucchini mix, roll, divide between plates and serve.

Nutrition: calories 290, fat 13.4, fiber 3.42, carbs 12.5, protein 6.9

Chicken with Peppers and Eggplant Pan

Preparation time: 10 minutes
Cooking time: 25 minutes
Servings: 4

Ingredients:
- 2 chicken breasts, skinless, boneless and cubed
- 1 red onion, chopped
- 2 tablespoons olive oil
- 1 eggplant, cubed
- 1 red bell pepper, cubed
- 1 yellow bell pepper, cubed
- Black pepper to the taste
- 2 cups coconut milk

Directions:
4. Heat up a pan with the oil over medium-high heat, add the onion, stir and cook for 3 minutes.
5. Add the bell peppers, toss and cook for 2 minutes more.
6. Add the chicken and the other ingredients, toss, bring to a simmer and cook over medium heat for 20 minutes more.
7. Divide everything between plates and serve.

Nutrition: calories 310, fat 14.7, fiber 4, carbs 14.5, protein 12.6

Balsamic Baked Turkey

Preparation time: 10 minutes
Cooking time: 40 minutes
Servings: 4

Ingredients:
- 1 big turkey breast, skinless, boneless and sliced
- 2 tablespoons balsamic vinegar
- 1 tablespoon olive oil
- 2 garlic cloves, minced
- 1 tablespoon Italian seasoning
- Black pepper to the taste
- 1 tablespoon cilantro, chopped

Directions:
1. In a baking dish, mix the turkey with the vinegar, the oil and the other ingredients, toss, introduce in the oven at 400 degrees F and bake for 40 minutes.
2. Divide everything between plates and serve with a side salad.

Nutrition: calories 280, fat 12.7, fiber 3, carbs 22.1, protein 14

Cheddar Turkey Mix

Preparation time: 10 minutes
Cooking time: 1 hour
Servings: 4

Ingredients:
- 1 pound turkey breast, skinless, boneless and sliced
- 2 tablespoons olive oil
- 1 cup canned tomatoes, no-salt-added, chopped
- Black pepper to the taste
- 1 cup fat-free cheddar cheese, shredded
- 2 tablespoons parsley, chopped

Directions:
1. Grease a baking dish with the oil, arrange the turkey slices into the pan, spread the tomatoes over them, season with black pepper, sprinkle the cheese and parsley on top, introduce in the oven at 400 degrees F and bake for 1 hour.
2. Divide everything between plates and serve.

Nutrition: calories 350, fat 13.1, fiber 4, carbs 32.4, protein 14.65

Parmesan Turkey

Preparation time: 10 minutes
Cooking time: 23 minutes
Servings: 4

Ingredients:
- 1 pound turkey breast, skinless, boneless and cubed
- 1 tablespoon olive oil
- ½ cup low-fat parmesan, grated
- 2 shallots, chopped
- 1 cup coconut milk
- Black pepper to the taste

Directions:
1. Heat up a pan with the oil over medium-high heat, add the shallots, toss and cook for 5 minutes.
2. Add the meat, coconut milk, and black pepper, toss and cook over medium heat for 15 minutes more.
3. Add the parmesan, cook for 2-3 minutes, divide everything between plates and serve.

Nutrition: calories 320, fat 11.4, fiber 3.5, carbs 14.3, protein 11.3

Creamy Chicken and Shrimp Mix

Preparation time: 10 minutes
Cooking time: 14 minutes
Servings: 4

Ingredients:
- 1 tablespoon olive oil
- 1 pound chicken breast, skinless, boneless and cubed
- ¼ cup low-sodium chicken stock
- 1 pound shrimp, peeled and deveined
- ½ cup coconut cream
- 1 tablespoon cilantro, chopped

Directions:
1. Heat up a pan with the oil over medium heat, add the chicken, toss and cook for 8 minutes.
2. Add the shrimp and the other ingredients, toss, cook everything for 6 minutes more, divide into bowls and serve.

Nutrition: calories 370, fat 12.3, fiber 5.2, carbs 12.6, protein 8

Basil Turkey and Hot Asparagus Mix

Preparation time: 10 minutes
Cooking time: 40 minutes
Servings: 4

Ingredients:
- 1 pound turkey breast, skinless, and cut into strips
- 1 cup coconut cream
- 1 cup low-sodium chicken stock
- 2 tablespoons parsley, chopped
- 1 bunch asparagus, trimmed and halved
- 1 teaspoon chili powder
- 2 tablespoons olive oil
- A pinch of sea salt and black pepper

Directions:
1. Heat up a pan with the oil over medium-high heat, add the turkey and some black pepper, toss and cook for 5 minutes.
2. Add the asparagus, chili powder and the other ingredients, toss, bring to a simmer and cook over medium heat for 30 minutes more.
3. Divide everything between plates and serve.

Nutrition: calories 290, fat 12.10, fiber 4.6, carbs 12.7, protein 24

www.ingramcontent.com/pod-product-compliance
Lightning Source LLC
Chambersburg PA
CBHW070407120526
44590CB00014B/1302